LAMPLIGHT ON COTTAGE LOAVES

Joan Kent

CENTURY · LONDON

Also by Joan Kent

Binder Twine & Rabbit Stew
Wood Smoke & Pigeon Pie
Hay Wains & Cherry Ale

First published 1993

1 3 5 7 9 10 8 6 4 2

© Joan Kent 1993

Joan Kent has asserted her right under the Copyright, Designs and
Patents Act, 1988 to be identified as the author of this work

First published in the United Kingdom in 1993 by Century Limited
Random House, 20 Vauxhall Bridge Road, London SW1V 2SA

Random House Australia (Pty) Limited
20 Alfred Street, Milsons Point, Sydney
New South Wales 2061, Australia

Random House New Zealand Limited
18 Poland Road, Glenfield
Auckland 10, New Zealand

Random House South Africa (Pty) Limited
PO Box 337, Bergvlei, South Africa

Random House UK Limited Reg. No. 954009

A CIP catalogue record for this book is available from the British
Library

ISBN 0-7126-5766-5

Typeset by SX Composing Limited., Rayleigh, Essex

Printed in Great Britain by Clays Ltd, St Ives Plc

Contents

Introduction

Time was when my country world revolved round a low-beamed farmhouse kitchen. Sooty-bottomed kettles made sibilant music on the hob of a log-stoked stove, and the loud-ticking pendulum of an ancient wall clock paced every second of passing time with ponderous footsteps.

As indifferent winter daylight faded into darkness, an oil lamp with a translucent fluted bowl took pride of place in the centre of a large cloth-covered whitewood table. A glass globe of rare beauty filled our mundane kitchen with patchwork patterns of muted colour, illuminating the beamed ceiling and workaday corners like rays of sunlight shining through the stained-glass windows of a church.

Tea time. Five feet nothing, perpetual motion in a floral pinny, my dumpling-shaped Mum presided over a fat brown earthenware teapot. Jars of home-made jam. Slabs of butter churned under protest. Lamplight on cottage loaves. Caraway seed buns, or wheel wedge slices of spiced fruit cake, and for those needing something more substantial, there was usually rabbit stew simmering in an oval iron pot at the back of the stove.

Born feet first into an Alice-through-the-looking-glass world, left-handed, left-footed and left-witted, I realized from that first day I spent with my left hand tied behind my back in a tiny village schoolroom, that everyone else was reading and writing their letters the opposite way round.

I was released from that torment by an old man who happened to be sharpening a hoe in our barn. He too had been 'born awkward'. With a piece of chalk, my father's shaving mirror, and the lid of the corn bin as an impromptu blackboard, he told me about mirror writing, emphasizing that I could overcome anything if I tried hard enough.

From that moment there was no holding me. Thanks to a far different schoolmaster, books became my salvation when the ground developed a nasty habit of coming up and hitting me, and I had to leave school at thirteen. The prescribed unpalatable diet for a lanky kid who had 'outgrown her strength' was raw liver sandwiches and half a cup of bullocks' blood daily. It must have worked. By my fourteenth birthday I was acting deputy midwife to a flock of sheep.

As the afterthought of a large family rich in everything but money, I watched the spaces widen around our kitchen table as my eight older brothers and sisters were married and had homes of their own. Comfort then was a home-made, hooked-rag hearthrug, a polished steel fender surrounding the whitestoned hearth, with a shining brass rail around it to warm winter chilblained feet.

With cherry wood fire logs flaring to the will of the wind in the chimney, my pipe smoking, my story-telling Dad would sit in his comfortable, rather than stylish, leather-covered armchair, relating tales with a rare ability to take the listener back to any time or place he chose. Inquisitive as the proverbial little pig with big ears, I listened to the oral history of agricultural labouring families, never realizing that such ephemeral accounts were as easily lost to memory as water droplets in dry sand.

We marvelled that the miracle of my brother's home-built wireless set could bring sounds of faraway foreign places into our insular little oasis of lamplight and log fires on cold winter nights.

The nine o'clock news was regarded as compulsory listening for my mother. We munched a supper of cold bread pudding and thick sustaining cocoa, the announcer's 'Goodnight Everyone' at the end of the bulletin convincing Mum that those nice-spoken gentlemen at the BBC concurred with her belief that half-past nine was the right time for sensible people to be getting upstairs to their beds.

Then came the moment to summon up enough courage to face that long solitary dash down the garden path, the stable lantern in my hand as reassuring as a pallid glow-worm against the encompassing rook-wing blackness of a moonless winter night. By prevailing standards, our unprepossessing lap-boarded privy was quite genteel, the boxed-in, craftsman-constructed mahogany throne boasting three smoothly rounded apertures of differing sizes, each with a delicately carved lid.

Common sense forewarned the inadvisability of a timid approach. Better by far to stamp one's feet on the cinder path and rattle that bootlace-strung latch before entering.

Creatures of the night had been known to seek shelter, gaining entry through the ill-fitting door of the bucket-emptying hatch at the back. Few predicaments were more stressful than to be quietly sitting contemplating personal matters, and hear a scrabbling rat scuttling in the dark recesses under the mahogany seat. Such wildlife could dramatically affect family social gatherings. The frivolities of a lively, overcrowded wedding reception, at which the guests seemed reluctant to depart from our house until the morning, was stopped short by my prodigious-sized Aunt Bet screeching as she stumbled back up the garden path, the lantern trembling and her voluminous salmon-pink bloomers in disarray around her ankles, the poor soul screaming that she had been attacked in the privy by a ferocious, snarling wild beast.

Big-game hunting with torches and a twelve-bore shotgun, Dad headed a men-only safari to the rear of the privy, flinging wide the hatch door. Disgruntled at having been disturbed in the only place to offer shelter after being accidentally shut out of his own hen run, Mum's best Rhode Island Red cockerel was precariously perched on the rim of the bucket, ready to peck anything that moved within reach of his long neck.

Then, of course, there was the unfortunate incident involving an inquisitive hedgehog. All in all it was wiser to cause a small commotion on after-dark sojourns to the 'outback' at the end of our garden path.

Another discipline to be endured prior to bedtime was a warm-water strip wash in an enamel bowl out in the stone-floored, draughty, back kitchen. White Windsor soap, a rough Turkish towelling flannel, and a roller towel that never quite reached where it was needed most.

An open window and an unheated bedroom was then considered essential for a healthy mind in a healthy body. Such attitudes made Great Britain great. My waste-not, want-not Mum scorned earthenware or rubber hot-water bottles as dangerous, expensive and totally unnecessary objects, prone to leaking stoppers. To her mind, the ideal bed warmer cost next to nothing and was totally trouble free. All one needed was an oven-heated brick and a fair-sized sock.

The flickering flame of my candle cast weird shadows on the staircase and long wide landing as I went to bed with my sock-covered source of alternative heating tucked under my arm.

Long practice made the swift transition from day clothes to nightgown a fine art in winter when my bedroom felt as chilly as a fishmonger's marble slab, with one well-worn sheepskin bedside mat offering the only refuge for chilblained feet on the icy lino-covered floor.

In an old house that creaked and sighed with every change of weather, it would have been easy to let imagination run amok when mice seemed to be rolling marbles above the ceiling, or when the fingertips of the copper beech tree boughs scratched the leaded panes of the side window and the wind whined down the chimney like lost souls crying to come in.

By daylight the front window offered picture-book views clear across country to the estuary and beyond. At night, the country darkness offered a bedside view of a galaxy of stars.

Never once did I regret staying at home to help my no-longer-youthful parents wrest a living from the land. Near-poverty, hard work, and occasional heartbreak was leavened with neighbourliness, a sense of purpose, and much laughter. Village life was never dull.

Introduction

I was blessed with a loving mother and father who never did a mean act in their lives, or turned anyone hungry or needing help from their door. To their memory I dedicate my world of long-forgotten summer hayfields, family gatherings, village concerts, muddy winters, log fires, lamplight on cottage loaves.

The Penny Whistle Man

'Be we all here then?' Albert Parsley enquires, checking our shivering numbers as we huddle in the shelter of the forge yard wall. Stamping numb Sunday-shod feet, we chatter like impatient magpies, anxiously aware that by Albert's infallible pocket watch the hired bus is almost half an hour overdue.

As instigator of this Rat and Sparrow Club excursion, committee member Tom Grommet makes a determined effort to boost morale, checking his list of names in the thin shaft of lamplight filtering through the undrawn blinds of Patience Cottage kitchen window. The two Miss Maristones glare their disapproval for such common-toned junketings, drawing the curtains with a contemptuous flourish, leaving us to the winter darkness of the night. On this last night of December with the old year dying, a raucous male minority chorus 'Goodnight

Sweethearts' and wish them a Happy New Year. Albert requests that we show a bit of decorum and order. Tom continues to tick off his pencilled register of names in the dim light of a borrowed cycle lamp, with the carbide running low.

No excursion Dolly Hackett embarks upon can stay straight-laced and gloomy. Lacking inhibitions, she publicly ascribes her immunity to the sub-zero temperature to the fact that she is wearing a pair of her husband's fleecy-lined long johns beneath the outfit she has made for this special outing. Confessing she has used the slightly naughty frilly garters that were part of her wedding-day attire to hoist the pants legs above her knee caps, she seeks assurance that the long johns are not visible below her coat hem. Somewhat sadly she admits that her garters, like herself, have slackened off considerably with the passing years, having a distinct tendency to droop. Ever helpful, Albert shines his lamp in the direction of Dolly's hemline, and offers his opinion.

'I reckon your breeching will stay hoisted, Doll, so long as you don't start jiggling about. I've got a bit of binder twine in my pocket, if that is any help.'

A small lad hurries along the village street, puffing and panting. Having run half a mile from Chappell's farm, he delivers a breathless message.

'Uncle Jim and Mr Dave say not to wait, because one of the cows fell on the ice in the yard at feed time, and they're mortal feared she is going to slip her calf. They say that if you can find someone to take their place, you might find me a shilling, or even sixpence, to make running down here to tell you worth my while.'

Albert gives him twopence for being a good boy. Other people copper hunt in their pockets and purses. Well compensated, the little lad goes off whistling in the dark.

Albert and Tom concur that it is now too late to offer anyone a free evening out, especially as it seems increasingly likely that we shall still be waiting for our transport by the forge yard wall when the old year lets in the new.

Lamps on village tea tables shine soft as winter glow-worms from the houses. Lenny Samkin waves to us from Duckett's Cottage, obediently waiting while his Aunt Ada prepares a single slice of bread and black treacle for his tea. This same fare frequently serves for his breakfast and dinner. Moon-faced, gentle

Lenny has a child-like mind in a man-sized body. But for the devoted ministrations and sheer determination of his penurious aunt, poor Lenny would have languished in the mental institution where she first found him as a very small child.

The Rat and Sparrow Club is a strictly masculine organization, the solitary exception being hefty Violet. Since no one ever recalls her wearing anything more feminine than riding breeches, hobnailed boots and leather gaiters, the validity of her membership is a situation that only the very brave would dare question or investigate. My proposal that Lenny and his Aunt Ada be invited to join us raises a point of order and causes some masculine debate. Bert, the blacksmith and club chairman, slips out of Forge House.

He settles the matter of the vacant seats by suggesting that a few of us nip across to ask old Ada if she would care to bring Lenny to the Rat and Sparrow Club outing.

A rumbling, rattling noise increases with every passing second. Dogs bark frantically, cottage doors open as the clanking, asthmatically engined charabanc lumbers along the village street, belching smoke. A morose little man, muffled in two overcoats, a balaclava helmet and steamed-up goggles, steps down from the cab, half-heartedly apologizing for his lateness, explaining the cause.

'I'm in all sorts of trouble,' he sighs sadly. 'I've come adrift underneath, and have a nasty suspicion that the end of my tail pipe dropped off along Plough Lane. The roads be that foggy and icy, I'm amazed that you daft beggars are willing to risk your necks riding behind me tonight. If you're still hellbent on destruction, some of you better cast around for a bit of wire and an old cocoa tin, and we'll try to bodge the old bus up again.'

Since there is no fog, Albert Parsley politely suggests that the driver would have better vision if he dispensed with his steamed-up goggles.

Confidence in the little man evaporates like hailstones in high summer as he concedes: 'Dang the pesky things, I clean forgot I was wearing them! I only put them on to stop my helmet slipping down over my eyes.'

Blacksmiths are ingenious by nature. While Bert, is getting busy around the nether regions of the bus, a few of us have persuaded Lenny and his Aunt Ada to put on their warmest coats.

3

This is only a matter of moments. By some remarkable feat, Ada always manages to keep them looking neat and tidy in the same clothes they have worn day in, day out, for years.

Walking to the bus, Ada admits that this will be the first time she has ventured out with Lenny after dark since she first brought him home to Duckett's Cottage as a small child.

With their task completed, Bert and his helpers wash their hands in the smithy water trough. Albert entreats everyone to hurry up and get aboard the bus. This is a twenty-six seater, we are thirty-eight in number and Big Bertha needs two seats, plus a generous amount of overhang space in the gangway.

'Scrunch up together, friendly like! Keep each other warm on the journey,' Albert advises.

All paws and green teeth, two of the leery Belton brothers attempt to persuade me to follow his advice by shouting, 'Come and sit with us, gal. We could warm you up a treat.'

Not for nothing are they known as 'handymen' in the village. Blushing angrily, I ignore their offer with a condescending glare and give them a wide berth.

The beer crates that materialize from behind the forge yard wall as if by magic clutter the bus gangway, but provide extra, somewhat precarious seating. My new half-crown silk stockings meet with instant disaster on their rough woodwork as I perch near Lenny and his aunt.

Lenny, clutching old Ada's hand, overwhelmed by this unexpected treat, fumbles into his pockets to bring out the penny whistle Tom Grommet made for him as a Christmas present. Smiling affectionately, his aunt dissuades him from giving a recital, remarking that she has had little peace or quiet since Christmas Day.

The icy road is as slippery as a wet eel skin. Those in the front seats tell us that they can see snowflakes falling by the faltering headlights of the bus. The solitary blue-tinted interior light flickers and dims considerably.

Issuing an ultimatum from the depths of his balaclava helmet, the driver announces that if he makes the proposed 'refreshment stop' at the Duck and Trumpet, it is highly unlikely that there is enough power in the bus battery to get the engine started again.

We are an hour behind schedule, so the majority agree that the idea is best abandoned, even if the Belton boys and a few of the Rat and Sparrow 'rowdies' act as if we are facing a long water-less drive across the sunbaked wastes of the Sahara, rather than the ordeal of a leisurely New Year's Eve trundle to a town just nine miles away.

We bumble cautiously along the icy lanes and through the outskirts of the town, approaching the main shopping centre area to find it still brightly lit with the Christmas illuminations and decorated Christmas trees. It is the first time Lenny has ever seen coloured electric light bulbs, and he cannot believe his eyes.

Having wiped off the steamy front window, the Rat and Sparrow Committee members occupying the first seats change places to give Lenny and his aunt a better view. Somehow in this snail-crawling mobile version of general post, I find myself pinned close to the window by an earthy smelling, male Belton body. I know now why my guardian angel prompted me to wear the high-heeled shoes that shocked my mother into predicting that I would have bunions and fallen arches before I was twenty-one. The spiky heel planted firmly on his shin does little to cool his ardour. I fumble around, feeling for the sharp hatpin Mum advised me always to carry in my handbag on these town excursions, but fail to find it.

Remembering another gem of motherly advice, I use the sharp corners of my handbag to great advantage as the bus lurches round the corner. The smelly lout grunts and gasps, muttering that he had only sat next to me as an act of kindness to a stuck-up, skinny beanpole, who would get no offers and end up as a withered old maid.

In my watchful state of armed neutrality, I fail to notice that Lenny's enthusiasm has made the driver miss his turning. We continue round four corners and come back through the fairy-light-lit square once again. Our setting-down point is a side street at the back of the Electric Theatre. Following Tom Grommet like a flock of sheep, we troop through the wrong entrance, wandering along a very grimy corridor until a startled-looking actor in a turban and striped bathrobe heads us off from adding to the crowded market scene on the stage.

'The curtain has been up for the last ten minutes,' growls a none-too-welcoming theatre manager, shush-shushing us through the foyer. Albert Parsley tells him that he is lucky we are here at all. His shrug of the shoulders and arm-waving gestures cut no ice with Albert.

With one withering glance he dismisses all these antics with the comment: 'There's no call for you to break out in a muck sweat, old matey. It's not our fault, and if you are going to act awkward, the Rat and Sparrow Club Committee won't book to come here again.'

We try to tiptoe into our places in the two front rows of the stalls, but Aladdin's Uncle Abanazar stops the show, sarcastically bidding us welcome. The silence is broken only by our minor shufflings and rearranging of places.

The Grounder and Drapper families, formerly good neighbours, are not now on speaking terms since Billy Grounder had his evil way with Maud Drapper. The fact that Billy is not yet twenty, while Maud has been twenty-five for the last ten years is immaterial. He's withstood the pressure to make her an honest woman, and been ungallant enough to suggest that the seduction was all on her side. To sit his mother next to Maud's parents could well lead to a small outbreak of civil war in the stalls.

I too apologize for being awkward, but there is no way that I will sit within arm's length of the three Belton brothers' six wandering hands. Suddenly all is silence, except for the sound of Tom Grommet's squeaking Sunday boots.

Still lost in wonder at their unexpected outing, Lenny and his aunt start discussing the street illuminations and all the decorated shop fronts, telling me they wouldn't have believed it to be real if they had not seen all those coloured electric lights with their own eyes. The irate audience behind us nudge our backs and tell us to keep quiet, but this is Lenny's first visit to any form of professional entertainment, and he wants to know what a pantomime is all about.

Except for the weeks of the pantomime season, the Electric Theatre is a cinema. Our front row seats mean we have to crane our necks to look up at the stage.

At this close range the actors' make-up looks grotesque. Widow Twankey's patched costume has huge sweat stains under each arm, and the only means of preventing the City of Old Bagdad being rent in two is a couple of large safety pins.

Lenny sits silent, his mouth wide open, his amiable moon face beaming, absolutely entranced. Abanazar, making magic and conjuring illusions, asks for a member of the audience to assist him in his act.

'You look a likely magician's apprentice,' he leers, beckoning to Lenny as he advances down the steps at the side of the stage. Lenny rises to meet him.

'No!' we say in anxious unison, but how do you explain to a packed theatre that inside Lenny's large lumbering body is the mind of a guileless, placid, four-year-old child. Tom Grommet, sitting on the far side of Aunt Ada offers to bring Lenny back to his seat, but she restrains him.

'If he shows any sign of being upset, I'll stop it. This is an experience he will talk of and remember all his life. Any sarcasm or clever talk will flow straight over Lenny and wash back on those that take advantage of his simple ways.'

Abanazar watches his moon-faced new assistant shambling towards him and makes some country cousin comment. The few uneasy twitters from the audience behind us are submerged by the concerted front-row boos.

Lenny's total lack of comprehension transforms Abanazar's magic act into a chaotic shambles. The audience believes that this is a clever comedy routine with Lenny as a plant. With the scripted scenario in total disorder, Abanazar plays along.

Lenny's friends sit taut with apprehension until Abanazar asks if he would like to win a prize by singing a song. Lenny needs no prompting, but starts the only piece of music he ever learned in all the wasted, miserable years he sat idly by the sand tray in the back corner of the village schoolroom. The clear treble soul of the hesitant child trapped in the twenty-years-old hulk of Lenny's body sings joyously through the first verse of 'The Ash Grove'.

We clap and stamp our feet, making the applause infectious. We realize that Lenny is singing again. The auditorium falls silent, listening to a haunting little song with simple words that are the philosophy of a trusting, happy little boy. He takes his penny whistle from his pocket and plays the tune again.

The stage is crowded with the cast, who stand applauding. We cheer and weep as Abanazar gently escorts Lenny back to his seat.

The house lights go up for an interval, and only then do we realize how grubby-looking are the men who helped Bert mend the bus exhaust pipe.

Most have dirt-smudged faces and blackened shirt collars, and those who washed their hands in the icy forge yard trough have found that the rusty water did nothing to help. Dolly Hackett has fared no better. In her enthusiastic support for 'Our Lenny', she has jumped up and down so much that her long johns and her famous blue garters are keeping each other company round her ankles, but this is our night out, and no one cares.

As the pantomime story reverts to the script, the cast seem to play their parts for Lenny. In the Grand Finale, Widow Twanky and Abanazar descend the Golden Palace staircase carrying a huge box of chocolates and a floral arrangement in a fancy beribboned basket. Advancing to the footlights, they present them to Lenny's surprised Aunt Ada. The whole theatre reverberates with cheers.

It is bitterly cold as we leave the theatre. Snowflakes drift lightly as duck down in the frosty air. We hurry to the restaurant for the fish-and-chip supper that is to round off our evening. Someone asks Lenny who taught him the new song he sang and played. He says that someone sings it inside his head.

It is late by our country standards, well past eleven, but the streets still throng with people waiting to welcome in the New Year of 1939. Aboard the bus we laugh and joke together.

Dolly Hackett's husband starts singing 'My Old Dutch' and some of us start speculating where we will be in forty, or even fifty years' time if old Hitler starts his nonsense. A three-inch layer of new snow covers the countryside as we skitter and skid home to the sleeping village.

Lenny and Ada go hand in hand to their cottage. I watch somewhat anxiously to see in which direction the Belton brothers are heading. Tom Grommet is astute enough to sum up the situation.

'Why don't you walk homewards with us, gal? 'Tis late for a girl to be out on her own.'

I wish them a Happy New Year as I leave them at their front gate, and walk on alone in bright moonlight that casts strange shadows under the edge of the wood, but makes the meadow almost as light as day. A love-lorn dog fox starts his melancholy serenading in the spinney up on Foxley Banks, and is answered by a vixen close at hand. A great white owl haunts along the lane hedge.

8

Tremulously I start whistling Lenny's little song, increasing my teetering, high-heeled pace to a stumbling run until I am safe within the back kitchen door of home.

Ted's Medal

Sturdier older boys had spent most of that dinner hour
sliding across the glassy surface of a large frozen puddle in
the centre of Foxley Parish School yard. Other smaller,
thinner-clad lads huddled with the girls in the scant shelter of
the school coal shed and toilet block at the end of the playground, mainly seeking sanctuary from the Arctic-spawned wind
until the clanking school bell allowed them to scuttle back into
school.

Whispered murmurings of three dozen country-booted pupils
settling down to afternoon lessons in the one communal classroom, became instant straight-backed silence as the schoolmaster entered, rapping the nearest desk with the steel ruler in
his hand.

The rigid disciplinarian, who had been appointed as Foxley
Head Teacher the previous Easter, was middle-aged, florid-faced,

the possessor of an extremely short-fused temper, forever deploring the fact that his wife's poor health had forced him to resign as deputy head of a large city school and take the far less prestigious post at Foxley, a hamlet miles from anywhere, having nothing to offer but fresh air.

Timorous as fieldmice fearing the sharp-eyed attentions of a hovering hawk, the children answered to assembly roll call, their ages ranging from doll-like, undersized Annie Arbott, not yet five and forever falling asleep in lessons, to gangling Ted Fordman, head and shoulders taller than his teacher, a few days short of his fourteenth birthday, then the statutory watershed for leaving school at the end of term. Amiable Ted encountered difficulties and discomfort in stowing his long legs under his desk, having outgrown the schoolroom in everything but academic skills and age.

Closing the blue-bound register with a flourish, the master glared in Ted's direction.

'On your feet, Fordman! Once again you have been dilatory and childish during the dinner hour, failing to attend to your responsibilities as Fire Monitor. Such idleness will be reflected in the reference report I will be expected to compose for you when you become a school leaver at the end of this winter term. This room is bitterly cold. Refill the coal scuttle and liven up the fire. You can also chalk up the afternoon roll call numbers on the registration board, thus informing any official visitors that a brilliant classical academic is doomed by circumstance to spend the next three hours like a swineherd, casting pearls of wisdom before thirty-six uncouth piglets.'

Incapable of tackling any task quietly, Ted lumbered along the gangway between the desks to take a large metal coal hod from the guard-protected fireplace that served as the only source of heating for the draughty schoolroom.

Bewildered by his instructions, Ted then collected a stick of chalk from the teacher's desk and asked if he was supposed to draw three dozen pigs on the roll board.

'Imbecilic lout!' the sarcastic mentor bellowed, glaring up at Ted towering above him. The remainder of the class inspected their desk tops with downcast eyes, aware that those of less stature were in imminent danger of feeling the stinging weight of the steel ruler around their ears. This weapon of punishment hurt just as much as the dreaded cane, but did not have to be entered in the *Record of Punishments*, a document inspected by the school governors against excessive or improper use.

Filled to the brim, the schoolroom coal hod held almost half a hundredweight, but Ted made light work of his task as he trailed a line of coal dust between schoolroom door and hearth.

His untidy thatch of raven-black hair habitually resembled the spilled contents of a discarded horsehair mattress, but now each tuft and spike was prematurely whitened with a sprinkling of snow. Large unmelted snowflakes clung to the shoulders and back of his shrunken jersey like plucked feathers as he attempted to revive the sulky, smouldering fire.

Torn between invoking the schoolteacher's rage and trying to convey the dangers of the prevailing weather to someone who had never experienced the ferocity of a Foxley winter, Ted went over to the teacher's desk and raised his hand.

'Please, sir, there's some terrible murky weather boiling up over the hills, and the wind has veered easterly. A long icicle has formed on the porch pump since dinner time. It's colder than a beggar boy's nose out there and littering down with snow. We are always sent home when weather sets in like this, sir, especially those with a long way to walk.'

Bowing to Ted with exaggerated sarcasm, the schoolmaster rapped on his desk to summon the immediate attention of the class.

'Pencil's down! Hands on heads and pay attention! Fordman here is going to give us a meteorological discourse and the benefit of his wisdom, or perhaps he is afraid he might melt like sugar at the first few flakes of snow. Pray continue, Fordman.'

Mumbling that he didn't know nothing about meteors or stars except for finding the North Star and 'Jack and his waggon', Ted's apprehension matured into desperation and the words came tumbling out.

'We get snowed in for a few days or even weeks every winter when the wind drifts the snow over the hills, sir. It's best that we go home.'

Incipient murmurs of approval for Ted's audacity were instantly stifled by a glacial all-encompassing glare, and the sight of the dreaded shiny steel ruler flashing around Ted's ears as he stumbled back to his seat.

'Do you really imagine you can trick me into dismissing school early, you ignorant idiot? No one leaves until four o'clock as usual. Now get back to your set work!'

The wild wind screamed around the schoolroom chimney top causing an occasional downdraught that belched sulphurous yellow smoke into the room. Most of the meagre warmth from the sullen stove was deflected from the pupils by the teacher's desk, placed close by the guard-railed hearth. By the end of the first lessen period, several small, shivering, bare-kneed children in 'the babies' group were whimpering with the cold.

'Indoor drill' was a form of exercise much practised in cold country classrooms as a means of stimulating juvenile circulation. This involved a considerable amount of jumping on the spot while flinging one's arms alternatively wide and round the body. Being taller than the rest, Ted could see through the bare patch in the ice-fronded, lattice-paned window as he leapt up and down. Disregarding the order to stop, he continued to jump like a demented toad, his right hand emulating a piston, to demand attention.

'Please sir, the snow has covered the top of the Brussels sprout row we planted in your garden, so it must be drifting deep up over the hill. We ought to go home instead of doing raffia work for the next hour and a quarter, especially the little kids. Some of us who live beyond Foxley End have close on a three-mile trudge home.'

'Sit down, you illiterate lout!' The apoplectic-looking master took a cane from a hook behind the cupboard door, making it swish and whistle as he advanced towards the anxious lad. Something in Ted's stance deterred him from actually hitting his largest pupil. In a voice high-pitched with rage, he announced that school would continue until the normal time for everyone but Ted, who would stay behind and axe logs into firelighting kindling wood in the school coal shed as a punishment for insolent indiscipline.

Ted had suffered many such detentions during the ten months since the 'new' schoolmaster's arrival. He was astute enough to realize that being detained for those log-splitting sessions invariably coincided with those times when the five-bushel kindling wood basket in the school-house scullery was almost empty.

Many children were now finding difficulty in working with

their raffia-threaded needles and lengths of unwieldly cane. When the teacher ordered everyone to get their coats from the dank icy lobby and return to their desks, it seemed that he had seen reason at last.

Thinking to help the others get home more quickly, Ted began packing away all the handicraft lesson materials, one or two other monitors following suit. For some unaccountable reason, these actions invoked the same type of sudden fury that Ted had once witnessed as a little lad when a normally placid bull turned rogue, tossing Ted's uncle out of the pen to leave the poor man lying in the mud with a permanently crippled back.

'Attention this instant!' the purple-faced teacher bellowed, lashing out at anyone unfortunate enough to be within striking distance. 'Hulking great baby that he is, lily-livered Fordman is afraid a few snowflakes will melt him. Those of you imagining him to be a clever rebellious spirit can contemplate that the coward's insolence has earned everyone an extra quarter of an hour in school. In a battle of wills, mine will prevail. Everyone will now continue with their work, and you will light the oil lamps, Fordman, before returning to your seat.'

A lull in the wailing wind seemed to encapsulate the schoolroom in an eerie moment of silence until a sound like stampeding cattle gradually increased to become an insistent drumming as the blizzard struck. The flat yellow light of the hanging oil lamp Ted had just lowered and lit, served to illuminate the 'infants' corner', where his stolid, six-year-old sister, Lucy, shared a desk with tiny Annie Arbott, one of two frail children living in the same isolated terrace of three farm cottages as Ted.

Annie's equally skinny brother, Ernie, was an undersized eight-year-old, prone to fits. He too looked blue and cold. It was often hard work getting them home when the weather was wet, or one or the other was feeling particularly tired or poorly. Ted knew that every minute they lingered in the classroom lessened his chances of reaching home safely in the gathering dark with a full-scale blizzard blowing outside. The three younger children were his responsibility. Scarlet-faced, he walked to the front of the desks, and in a voice that wavered between treble and baritone, called to Lucy, Annie and Ernie.

'To hell with it! We're going home.'

The three smaller children began to walk towards him, hesitating as the teacher's cane sliced through the air before making contact with the thin jersey covering Ted's back and shoulder blades. Head and shoulders taller than his tormentor, Ted promised he would stuff the cane down the schoolmaster's throat if it was used again that afternoon. Digging deep into un-dreamed-of powers of intellect, he warned that he now held the schoolmaster totally responsible for the safety of all the children put at risk by not being allowed out of school before the blizzard struck.

In a silence so profound that Ted could hear the round-faced clock ticking away on the schoolroom wall, he watched the two little girls and Ernie come forward. Slowly he led them out. His placid, pixie-hooded little sister was reasonably wrapped up against the winter weather, having leather gaiters and calf-length boots to protect her feet and legs.

He had an old army greatcoat that had once belonged to his bull-gored, bed-bound uncle, and a hat, hand-knitted by his Granny from a tea cosy pattern gone wrong. They both had Christmas present scarves, knitted by the old lady from odd-ments of wool, nothing to boast about, but surprisingly warm. The two Arbott children were not half as well protected, Ernie's stick-thin legs chapped red raw between his short, patch-seated trousers and droopy undarned socks that sagged into down-at-heel, broken boots.

Frail Annie was going to be Ted's main problem. The snow on the porch step was already deeper than her shoes. Each falling snowflake seemed to gravitate towards the safety-pinned tear that had been in the little girl's coat since she had fallen into a bram-ble bush the previous blackberry-picking season. Ted tied his own scarf around her head, taking the ends across her chest to tie like a bustle at the back. It needed a lot of brotherly persuasion before Lucy reluctantly relinquished her own 'comforter' scarf to shivering Ernie as soon as they were safely out of the school gates.

Ted realized that the children were in no fit state to face the blizzard conditions of the three-mile walk home over the exposed hilly roads. The safer way would be the valley bridle path that was usually ankle-deep in winter mud. Daylight was fading fast. The whimpering little girls stumbled along between Ted and stoical young Ernie as they followed the footpath down across the meadows. When Annie slipped over in the snow, too fatigued to be able to stand, Ted had no alternative but to pick her up and carry her, assuring Lucy and Ernie that they would all feel warmer when they reached the valley track and the shelter of the yew grove along the edge of the woods.

Having achieved this objective, Ted felt so totally exhausted that he almost yielded to their pleas to sit down and rest on a clear patch of ground under the snow-laden canopy of yew boughs. Common sense prevailed. If they lingered here in the intense cold, young Annie could easily freeze to death. He must drive them on and not let them go to sleep.

Fear changed his voice: 'Stay awake, stop whining, and do as I say or I'll clear off home without you!'

The sheer terror on Annie's pinched little face made him change his tone to give a realistic impression of their peppery-tempered schoolmaster.

'Class will sing "Land Of Hope And Glory" when I give the note, then keep walking and singing until I give permission to stop!'

Ted had once read a book about Himalayan mountain climbers overcoming fatigue and frostbite by singing to keep themselves awake and moving until they reached base camp. His objective, Badlock's Hatch, known as Badlocks, lay about a mile farther along the valley track. This small, semi-derelict stone building had a tin-patched roof and boarded-up windows, serving the purpose of a farm storeshed.

In earlier times it had been a gamekeeper's cottage, until the last occupant either hanged himself or was murdered by poachers, old Badlock being believed by some to haunt the valley at the time of the full moon, still looking for the perpetrators of this dastardly deed.

According to Gran Best, the toothless old lady who lived in the cottage between Ted's home and that of Mrs Arbott, Annie and Ernie's mother, Gran's own father had discovered the unfortunate Badlock swinging from the gun rack beam, suspended by the copper wire from which he made rabbit snares.

Having cut the victim down, Gran Best's father apparently realized that there was no box, chair or stool near the beam for anyone with suicidal tendencies to jump from, and as Gran explained, you just can't hang yourself with both feet on the floor.

Gran's father was warned to keep his opinions to himself if he wanted to keep his estate worker's tied cottage and job, but common conjecture linked the illustrious estate owner's black sheep gambler cousin with the incident. He had been seen in a public house stable yard some ten miles distant on the previous evening, deep in conversation with four notoriously violent poaching brothers. He was Malaya-bound on an indefinite stay with a tea-planting associate before a coroner could decide that the unfortunate Badlock should be consigned to an unmarked suicide's grave in the unconsecrated patch of ground on the north side of Lockley churchyard.

Gran Best's spooky tales about Badlocks had been enhanced by reported sightings of eerie lights. Ted's Dad dismissed such talk as hogwash, the supposed sightings being nothing more than the activities of vagrants seeking shelter along the old green way as they walked from one workhouse to the next.

Ted hoped his Dad was right, but also that no tramp had chosen to stay there for the coming night because Lucy and Ernie could scarcely drag one foot in front of the other, and little Annie now felt like a ton weight on his back.

'Come on, kids! When we get to Badlocks you can rest while I find some of the old sacks that are laying around in there to wrap round us and keep us warmer for the rest of the way home.'

Half a mile farther along the snow-covered valley track, the derelict old cottage, all entwined around with ivy, had galvanized sheeting nailed across the rotting empty window frames, and a makeshift door secured by the latch with string.

By the time Ted reached this unlikely-looking haven, he was literally carrying all three younger children and feeling so unbelievably weary that he wondered how much longer his trembling legs would support his weight. He knew he could not go on. With dusk descending and the raging Arctic gale still hurling snow across the valley, Ted cut the frozen latch string with his penknife.

The interior was as black as midnight, but with the door closed the respite from the icy wind made it easier to draw breath.

Stumbling around in the dark, with three frightened youngsters clinging to him, Ted found a heap of straw bales. The farmer owning this storage shed would probably belt him for scattering the straw, but he could deal with that later. Annie, Lucy and Ernie needed no persuasion to shed their snow-caked, frozen top layers of clothing to nestle down as easily as little piglets burrowing beneath the dry warm straw.

In ordinary circumstances Badlocks was forbidden territory. Ted's only previous peep inside the old cottage was on the occasion he had been invited to join some older lads in an illicit, sick-making, home-made hog-weed cigarette-smoking session, undertaken in the glorious warmth of a hayfield- and honeysuckle-scented night.

Remembering that experience, Ted recalled that there was an old chimney place on the far wall, and a heap of half-rotted hazel thatching spars in the corner. The box of school lamp-lighting matches that he had forgotten to replace in the schoolmaster's desk was still in his jersey pocket. He offered reassurance.

'If I can get a fire going, we'll be far safer here until the blizzard dies down.'

His words were wasted on the others. All three had fallen into deep exhausted sleep. Ted knew nothing about hypothermia, but he was aware that an undernourished mite like Annie could well freeze to death. The appalling possibilities of their situation so overwhelmed him that he felt warm tears running down his cold face.

Shivering uncontrollably, he felt around and found a bundle of potato sacks, which he spread over the straw under which his young companions were sleeping before wriggling down beside them, never imagining that he too would almost immediately succumb to deep dreamless sleep.

He woke as Lucy stirred restlessly beside him. The blizzard had died away, and in the pitch black silence, he realized that little Annie was crying in her sleep. Ernie, who had lain cradling his little sister in his arms, began to make strange snorting noises. Annie's small plaintive voice complained that he had wet his breeches, casually adding that this usually happened just before he went into a fit.

Ted had often seen Ernie's mother deal with this situation, but this time there was no wooden spoon to place between his grinding teeth, no tin bath of tepid water to relax the thin, rigid arched back. All Ted could muster from his pockets was the mouth organ bought from the sixpenny stores as a twelfth birthday present. He forced this prized possession between Ernie's clenched jaws, each spasm making its own rasping tune.

As the fit passed, the two weeping little girls entwined arms around the inflicted body as he subsided into a trance-like sleep. Lucy now complained that she was hungry, thirsty, and uncomfortable because there were round lumpy things under the straw. Ted delved beneath her and realized that they were lying on a mound of potatoes, the straw bales being a protection against the frost.

He took the box of matches out of his jersey pocket and opened it with trembling, cold-numbed hands. His clumsy fingers encountered nothing. He had been holding the box upside down and the precious matches had fallen like proverbial needles in a haystack amongst the straw. Warning the girls to stay absolutely still, he spent an eternity of minutes carefully feeling the straw stalks, but only managed to find four matches. Feeling faint with cold and disappointment, Ted stood up, working his way forward until his fingers touched brickwork. His face brushed against a dead creeper as he stumbled and fell. Glancing up, he realized that he was now sitting in the chimney place, for there, high above, was a patch of moonlight and a bright star.

With a handful of dead ivy twigs and dry straw he could kindle a fire, provided that the precious matchbox was not damp. The first two matches were useless, the third spluttered, fluttered and offered a small gleam of light sufficient to set the tinder-dry dead ivy alight. The bundle of thatching rods made a blaze that gave Ted enough light to find more fuel. As he was breaking up a worm-eaten old wall cupboard he found the stump of a candle some vagrant had inadvertently left behind.

'You can stop your snivelling now,' Ted told the little girls. 'We'll have baked spuds for supper, and we can melt some snow in that old cocoa tin. If we warm those sacks, you can climb into them and you'll be snug as fleas on a dog's back here for the rest of the night, while I keep the fire going.'

Ted kept vigil, aware that drifting snow had piled up higher than the tin-covered windows, but that was something the little ones did not need to know.

Furious that the stubborn city-bred schoolmaster had failed to send his pupils home after morning lessons, despite the worsening weather, many Foxley parents were determined that he would never have the opportunity to put young lives at risk again.

Lantern-carrying villagers had been out all night digging along the lanes too deep in snow for horse-drawn snowploughs to tackle, searching for the four children still missing. In sub-zero temperatures and with hope fading as dawn came, the men were frantically clearing a drift on the hill when someone said he could smell roast potatoes. Another man noticed a thin spiral of smoke rising from the old fodder store of Badlocks in the valley half a mile away.

Ted's bravery and common sense was praised by everyone but the schoolmaster, who accused him of being a thief. On the first morning Ted returned to school, the teacher told his pupils that only ignorant country yokels would make a hero out of a lout who had purloined school property, namely a box of matches.

Ted stood his ground.

'They weren't pinched, only borrowed. You ain't caning me no more. It is you who should be punished. You could have had at least three little 'uns killed.'

The schoolmaster looked up at Ted towering above him, then glanced at the solitary headless match in the crushed box and sat down at his desk.

When Ted brought the three youngsters home from school that afternoon, Gran Best called him into her kitchen and handed him a small box.

'Yere you be, boy. It belonged to my father and his father before 'un, won in some old war for bravery. I don't reckon anyone deserves to have this more than you.'

There would be other wars in which Ted would be awarded other decorations, but Gran Best's medal remained the proudest possession of his life.

Lizzie and the Rats

The parish council meeting, held at the village hall, was scheduled to start at 7.30. With customary rural disregard for punctuality, the only councillors converging on the converted army hut by eight o'clock, were farmer Harry, and butcher Cecil Snobbert.

Arriving together, they stood waiting for the custodian of the hall keys to emerge from her cottage across the green, carpet-slippered and complaining.

Two other people, not involved in council deliberations, approached along the lane. Lizzie Buckerby, a formidable matron, was Sunday-hatted and wore a look of grim determination. Some few paces behind came her husband, looking sheepish, obviously wishing he was back indoors with his boots off for the night.

Conversing quietly, Harry and Cecil tried to surmise the

21

couple's destination, wondering which lucky people were to be subjected to an evening with Lizzie Buckerby's sharp tongue. To their surprise, Lizzie stopped, silently sniffing her displeasure at the locked hall door, then marching across the road to perch herself on the footpath stile in the opposite hedge, imperiously beckoning Bodger to follow suit.

In a feeble attempt to disguise his discomforture, Bodger called, 'Evening, Harry! Evening, Gristle!'

'Gristle' was the unfortunate nickname accorded to the butcher whose scraggy cuts of beef, lamb, pork or mutton were at total variance with the legend 'Purveyors Of Best Quality Meat Only', which appeared above his shop door and was sign-written on a board fronting the basket carrier of Cecil Snobbert's delivery tricycle. Gristle's three wheeler was something of a challenge to local lads, being reputedly notoriously difficult to ride. In consequence, it was often 'borrowed' and almost as frequently bent by daring lads believing they could ride down the steep bends on Lockley Hill on this unwieldy steed.

Aware that it was a source of temptation, Gristle duly chained it to a nearby tree and, glancing across at the Buckerbys, asked Bodger if he intended to revive old memories by doing a bit of courting on the stile as soon as Harry, himself, and the rest of the council members were inside the parish hall. Bodger smiled lugubriously in denial.

'That's like asking a short-sighted chap who can't swim to walk across a broken footbridge over an icy flooded river when he's done the same thing once before and darned near drowned!'

Lizzie's reaction to this observation was a swift jab in the solar plexus, leaving Bodger too short of breath for further words to be exchanged.

Gristle was bemoaning the caretakers non-appearance when that lady arrived, indignant that he had not ridden across on his tricycle to collect the keys himself. Nobody cared that she was working herself into an early grave, keeping the hall clean for half-a-crown a time, her with her poor Gilbert's carbuncle to poultice, and never a chance to sit with her feet in a bowl of warm water, soaking her wretched corns.

This doom-laden monologue was cut short by Lizzie Buckerby calling her a miserable old moaner, and asking pointedly of everyone in general what time the meeting was supposed to start.

Harry's comment that if it had started on time, it would by now be almost over, galvanized Lizzie into activity, advancing across the road, dragging Bodger with her as if he was a recalcitrant donkey on a very short rein.

'Right then! Get that door open and let a body sit down comfortable like! Bodger and me are here as public specked taters, as they say on the wireless. So what happens now then?'

'Nothing much!' This seemed to be the only honest answer Harry could give her. The malodorous staleness of the hall embodied years of tobacco smoke, coke fumes, French chalk, sweaty humanity, and dust of ages in unswept corners, and the mildewed dampness of winters past. The solitary spluttering hanging lamp, low on oil, and smoking, did nothing to improve the atmosphere with its sickly yellow light.

One of the assembling councillors, now five in number, suggested that the meeting be adjourned to Four Oaks Barn because the tenant there had invited friends and helpful neighbours to join in his supper celebrating Harvest Home.

Gristle thought this could well be out of order, and pointed an indicative thumb towards Lizzie and Bodger Buckerby sitting on a lonely island of two chairs in the middle of the floor.

'They're not council members, so they shouldn't be here!' argued the man who had suggested that the elected representatives of the public could discuss local matters more thoroughly with a wedge of veal and ham pie and a jar of Four Oaks cider in their hands.

Blacksmith Bert was convinced that some ruling or other allowed parishioners to attend, so long as they kept quiet and took no part in the proceedings. He tried to remember when a member of the public last attended a meeting, and asked the couple why they had come.

As Lizzie stood up, folding hefty arms across an impressive bosom, farmer Harry realized that her Sunday hat rated her presence as an occasion of some importance. She had even made Bodger shave mid-week.

This was contrary to his custom of only coming into close contact with his cut-throat razor once a fortnight, Bodger's argument being that scraping away at a few fine whiskers before they were firm bristles was like trying to snip away at blades of new grass with nail scissors instead of mowing a full crop of hay.

Harry's repetition of Bert's reasonable enquiry about the couple's presence was dismissed by Lizzie's forthright answer: 'Rats!'

The uncertain silence, caused by councillors wondering if this was an angry retort or statement of fact, was broken by the arrival of the sixth councillor, apologetic and untidy in appearance, his late arrival being caused by a sow that had just given birth to thirteen live piglets. The reeking pig muck plastering his boots justified the validity of his excuse.

After accepting the congratulations of all of those present, he considered the small number of councillors gathered asking, 'Do we have a quorum?'

Gristle, anxious to get the meeting started, said they had never bothered with things like quorums before, and were not interested in such new-fangled gadgets now. If the meeting would come to order, the minutes of the last one could be read. Seeing that there was nothing of importance in them, and that he could not read them without his wife's spectacles, he proposed that they be taken as read.

There was not much 'Any other business' to concern them apart from old Miss Ashstead again demanding that Chappell's dairy herd be prevented from depositing 'pancakes' on the road as they went back and forth along Millers Lane for milking twice a day. The barmy old dame had sent ten shillings to help fund 'preventative measures'. Perhaps someone present would volunteer to personally refund her money and explain that cattle could not be house-trained or made to wear nappies, nor could Dick the roadman play pat-a-cake with his shovel in Millers Lane four times a day.

'That's it then! I now close the meeting!' Gristle concluded in his best presiding manner.

Red-faced and looking as if steam might well soon hiss from her ears, Lizzie bellowed, 'No you don't, you great lummock! Bodger here wants to know what you are going to do about our rats!'

Bodger was hauled to his feet, nonplussed and mumbling. Lizzie pushed him back into his seat and repeated the question.

'Me?' Gristle asked in mystification. 'I'm a butcher, not a pied piper, missus.'

Lizzie retorted that she would not be surprised at anything he put into his sausages. She intended to stay where she was until she had a satisfactory answer. It was bad enough to see rats rolling eggs from the backyard henhouse across the yard. She had suffered a nasty experience while minding her own business in the privy, and at night rats cluttered about in the roof space as if they were wearing jackboots, as Bodger could confirm, except that as soon as his head hit the pillow, it was as if she had a lump of cold suet pudding in her bed. The invitation for anyone present to listen in her bedroom for themselves was hastily declined. Lizzie said the village rubbish dump over at Petty Dane caused all her troubles.

Legend held this strangely eerie place to have been the entrance to an underground cavern where the native inhabitants hid their harvest grain from invaders in the unrecorded days of history.

The more realistic explanation held the strand hollow in the ground to be the effect of a schism in the underlying rock formation. Generations of villagers had attempted to fill it in with rubbish that sank down, always leaving room for more.

A suggestion that the sanitary inspector be consulted made Lizzie squawk that people would imagine she had bedbugs and other crawlies if he came to her door.

Trying to calm the situation, farmer Harry told of his recent conversation with Dick the roadman, who had reported seeing dozens of rats crossing Petty Dane Lane towards his farm fields and buildings. Apparently Dick's wife had a mole catcher up-country cousin, who claimed he could clear rats from anywhere, given free lodgings, free beer, shelter for his pony and a few quid in his pocket.

Dick's large family were already packed like sardines in a tin in his two-bedroomed cottage, ruling out having his wife's cousin as a temporary lodger, but he was sure the mole catcher would be pleased to help, given somewhere to stay.

'If he makes it possible for me to go to the privy in peace, he can stay with us, so long as you chaps pay for his board and lodgings,' Lizzie answered, and after a few more details were settled the informal meeting was closed.

Contented that her mission had been accomplished, Lizzie went home with Bodger, looking forward to a bit of company when their rat-catching lodger came.

Jaunty in his moleskin waistcoat and trousers, the lively little man arrived a week or so later, two smooth-haired terriers sitting beside him in his pony cart.

He received two weeks' fees funded by the parish, proving his success by the hundreds of rats' tails nailed to a board on a pole by Bodger's gate. Word spread that the chirpy little man was an expert. His skills became in such great demand that Lizzie went along to help him at the flour mill, various granaries and farms, as well as over at the rubbish tip.

Being none too happy with the situation, Bodger consulted Gristle in his capacity as council chairman, only to be informed that in his lodger's estimation the job of exterminating the thousands of rats over at the rubbish tip would take several more weeks.

Gristle admitted unofficially that this was causing some financial embarrassment to the parish council.

Bodger answered bluntly that he knew an unofficial and cheaper answer to their problem, if Gristle cared to help.

So it was that on All Saints' Eve the night was made eerie by a strange glow coming from Petty Dane way, Gristle and Bodger having set alight to the ancient pit with a barrel of tar.

The rats disappeared as if by magic. so did the little man with the moleskin waistcoat, taking Lizzie with him.

Far from being disconsolate, Bodger was of the opinion that the twenty pounds that the rat-clearing operation cost had been the best use of public money the council had ever sanctioned, even if the old rubbish tip smouldered on for years.

Onions make me cry

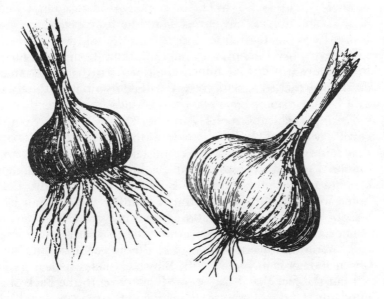

I was nine years old, helping the schoolmaster's wife make rhubarb jam, when her preserving pan slipped on the stove and caught alight, setting the schoolhouse chimney on fire. Being too young and stupid to help clear up, I scooted home early, taking the short cut through the woods, heavy-scented with bluebells, then on across Stoney Field where the warm wind rippled the young wheat like sea waves sweeping across the bay.

The back door of our old farmhouse was seldom closed during the days of summer. Any of the barnyard fowls that dared approach the threshold were taught their manners by the two domineering tortoiseshell cats that lay sleeping on the doormat as I entered, calling the age-old cry of every returning school-child: 'Mum! Where are you, Mum? I'm home.'

There was an ominous 'unlived-in' silence. I searched up and down through all the rooms, even venturing up into the attics, disused since farm servants lived like slaves on board wages, and plucked up courage enough to look down the old wine cellar where Mum experimented with trying to grow mushrooms in the dark.

Failing to find her, filled with intuitive fear, I ran through the farm buildings, crying and calling. I knew that Dad and my brothers, Stan and Harold, were timber hauling in Church Woods, and none of my sisters would be back before tea time. Just as I was feeling frantic, I saw her in the old walled garden, sitting with her back towards me on an old hen coop. She was leaning forward, looking limp as a rag doll that had shed its saw-dust. I approached unnoticed and realized that Mum was sobbing as if her heart must break.

Fearing some catastrophe, I ran howling to her arms, but she wiped my face on her floral pinafore, then tried to convince me that her eyes were red because she had been peeling Spanish onions. I was all too ready to believe her. She alone had kept a cheerful face when my brother Billy suddenly decided to leave home and lodge with his sweetheart's family. The rest of us wept for our quiet bookworm brother, but my dry-eyed Mum ex-pounded the belief that children needed to stretch their wings, and parents must learn to love and let them go. In finding lovely Grace and her family to be with, Billy had made an ideal choice.

I put the fact that I had seen Mum crying to the back of my mind until all ten of us were sitting round the tea table, and I saw the same ashen, stricken expression on her face. Bent almost double, she protested that it was just a spasm. Realizing there were no onions for our meal, I spoke up about the incident that afternoon.

The look Mum gave me made me feel like a Judas, but my sister Eve told me off for not mentioning it before. Having been a member of the ambulance brigade for three months, Eve was considered something of a medical expert. She was sure that Stan or Harold should drive Mum to the city doctor in our solid-tyred, ancient 'Tin Lizzie' lorry, and this caused some discussion about which one would drive. Stan had been known to notch up forty-five miles an hour and would get there faster, but with Harold being the steadier driver, Mum would get there in better shape. In the event, all the rest of the family except June went with her. June stayed behind and packed me off to bed.

It was incredible to wake and find no Mum, and no breakfast ready. My sisters were short on words and temper as they rushed round getting ready to cycle to their city jobs, but there was a pall of silence about the place, as if all the clocks had stopped. All I asked for was some breakfast, and the chance to slip upstairs and see Mum before I went to school, but everyone evaded my questions.

There seemed scant hope of the first, so I went up to Mum's bedroom. It was empty and the bed had obviously not been slept in all night. Eve was pumping air into her bike tyre as I ran downstairs, frantic with unanswered questions.

Avoiding my eyes, she said jerkily, 'Stan's in the cowshed. He'll explain what is going on.'

With the peak of his cap turned sideways, and his head against the flank of a stubborn old shorthorn, Stan paused from his milking, saying, 'Didn't the girls explain that Mum is terribly ill and has had an operation in hospital? Dad and Harold are still with her, and the rest of us were there half the night. You are to stay with Grace's family where Billy is lodging, so you won't get homesick. Collect a few clothes and I'll take you over there as soon as I finish this.'

I had never been away from home before and pleaded to stay, but Stan said I would be a nuisance and get in the way. Having stuffed a jumble of my clothes in an old rush bag, I stood waiting with all the enthusiasm of a dockside convict ready to be transported to Botany Bay.

The metal carrier above the rear mudguard of Stan's rattling bike was an uncomfortable means of transport. I was crying for my Mum, and for all that he was eleven years older, Stan sniffled as much as I did all five miles of the way.

I knew Grace's home only from the roadside view of old chimneys and a pan-tiled roof behind a ten-foot, red-brick wall, but as Stan pushed open a solid wooden garden gate, I saw a sun-soaked old house with wisteria, honeysuckle and roses climbing to the eaves.

Red tulips lined the paved garden like guardsmen, and banks of yellow wallflowers filled the air with their homely scent. Grace came out to greet us, instantly offering her understanding that I was feeling utterly rejected and alone. The house was so impressively uncluttered, with old carved furniture, and carpets on the floors instead of lino, that I asked Grace if her father was some kind of lord.

Patiently Grace explained that her home had once been the Dower House when a noble family owned the vast estate. When their line ran out the place was left to their church. The mansion had become a training college for priests, but now it was unused and rapidly deteriorating. There was the possibility that the estate would be put up for sale, but until that happened, her father was still the steward, determined to make the place earn some part of the vast expense of upkeep in various ways.

Grace's mother was a tiny gentle-faced lady, her father a broad-shouldered man with a mane of white hair and a booming voice. He said that I had no more meat on my bones than a winter-starved sparrow, but I liked the way his eyes crinkled. Then, just when my spirits were lowest, watching Stan's departure, my brother Billy came in, hugging me, hauling along a grey-muzzled old collie on the end of a twenty-foot-long rope.

'This is Bess, Jo,' he said by way of introduction. 'She is losing her sight but needs exercising, so you can help us look after her. You can roam anywhere you like inside the wall and Bess will bring you back here. Stay away from the lake edge where it runs deep by the beech trees, but otherwise you can come and go as you please.'

The glorious truth dawned on me that I was not expected to go to school. Leading the ambling old collie at a snail's pace, I wandered along winding paths through the overgrown parkland, with cedars, statues and small shrines screened by flowering bushes and blossoming shrubs.

Billy was working in a vast greenhouse shaded by ancient vines. The mansion itself was a huge stone building that looked impressive from a distance, until one noticed the cracks in the crumbling walls. The day passed quickly, my homesickness subdued by the interest of my new surroundings, but it came back in vast sweeping waves as soon as I was sent to bed in a small white-walled room. It was sparsely furnished, just a bed, a chair and a huge crucifix on the wall.

I snivelled myself to sleep, and woke weeping for my mother. Somewhere outside the open latticed window a nightingale was pouring its heart out, and moonlight shone upon the crucifix on the wall. The agony on the carved face seemed so realistic, I was sure it watched me, and I scuttled out of bed to find my brother's room just along the landing. Awkward as ever, I knocked a small table flying, and Billy found me sitting on the landing floor nursing my bruised leg.

He took me back to my room where my fears poured out of me like liquid from an uncorked bottle. I was sure our Mum was dying, wanted to be back home in my own bed, and was unnerved by the crucifix on the wall. Billy took the chair across to the window and pointed to the lights of the city way down in the valley.

Pinpointing a group of lights, he told me that if I could see the second small light on the third storey up, I was looking at the hospital room where our Mum was lying, so she was not so far away after all. He went downstairs and came back with the old collie dog to keep me company, and tucked me in for the night.

As soon as he was gone, I was out of bed, looking through the window towards the hospital lights in the valley, making sure that the lamps in Mum's room were not turned out. I woke on the bedside mat with the collie beside me. There was dawn mist across the city, but I could see Billy walking towards the greenhouse down below.

Dressing quickly, I ran down to find him, desperate for my own kind. I helped him gather salad crops for the morning market, then went in to breakfast with him. Grace's mother was presiding over a great pan of eggs and bacon, but stopped to kiss me good morning.

'There's good news from the hospital. Your mother is improving. Grace is going to spend the day showing you all over the estate so that you will feel at home here during the six or so weeks before your mother comes out of hospital. Now you are not feeling homesick or unhappy, are you, Jo?' she asked kindly.

'Oh, no,' I snivelled. 'I have been helping Billy pull spring onions, and onions always make me cry.'

With breakfast cleared, gentle Grace suggested that we extended her guided tour of my new surroundings. We took my unlikely-looking guard dog with us, docile shaggy old Bess ambling along on the end of a long slack rope lead. Set against the backcloth of wooded hills, the façade of the vast stone-built mansion seemed dilapidated in bright morning sunlight. A front vista of terraced lawns and formal box-hedged gardens led down to an ornamental lake where huge golden carp played hide and seek amid the lily pads.

Multi-coloured rhododendrons and azaleas bloomed along the paths, and at the end of an avenue of ancient beech trees there stood a tiny twelve-sided chapel, each wall having a stained-glass window depicting one of the Disciples. Within the low wall surrounding this sombre spot were a dozen mossy gravestones, the Latin inscriptions upon them eroded by time and weather. For all that the sun was shining and the temperature well into the seventies, there was an icy cold atmosphere of indescribable sadness that made me shiver with apprehension.

I wanted to hurry away, but Grace laid a gentle reassuring hand on my shoulder, pointing to a plain little brown bird in a nearby hawthorn bush.

'Stay still a minute, Jo,' she whispered. 'There is a nightingale. Everyone knows that nightingales will only sing in happy places and they come back here every summer. Did you not hear them singing to tell you all would be well with your Mum last night?'

She almost managed to allay the uneasy sensation that was raising my crop of goose pimples. Maybe she was right. If nightingales flew halfway across the world to sing close by the little chapel, there could not possibly be anything supernatural or strange about the place.

We wandered through the lower floor of the great house by way of a small side door leading in from a back courtyard, but we heard the yard bell at the Dower House ringing for our midday meal, and hurried back.

I was puzzled by the way Grace's family gave thanks for their meal with hand signals and a foreign language, but Billy said this was no time for theological discussions and told me to shut up.

He was taking Grace to see Mum for an hour or two, so I was to behave myself, keep the old collie with me wherever I wandered and come back if I heard the yard bell ring. When they left I tried to do some left-handed knitting, but produced nothing but a cat's cradle of wool. The old dog was restless, so we wandered out across the park.

With her rope lead at full length, she led me through a sunken rock garden, down along the lake edge, where wild watermint and yellow iris grew and moorhens squabbled, then up across the wide grass terrace in front of the old house. Skirting the walls, we ended up in the courtyard where Grace had taken me that morning. Bess was panting with the heat, so I tried to get her some water from a pump in the yard.

Needing two hands, I put Bess's rope lead under my foot, but she tugged it free and shot off through the iron grating of a broken basement window. I did not fancy following her into the gloom, so I went in through the doorway, calling loudly, with only the echo of my voice to answer back.

I walked through two or three rooms, opening doors in case they led to the basement into which Bess had vanished, and eventually came to the bottom of a narrow flight of stairs. I called again, and was sure I heard Bess padding about overhead. I went up, passing through a succession of rooms, some with fireplaces and doors missing, others with wormy-looking old furniture and moth-eaten curtains still hanging at the windows.

By the time I reached the front of the house and the first-floor landing of the impressively grand main staircase that swept up towards a great glass dome above roof level, I found there was a marvellous view down across the city, except that a copper beech tree in the park just screened my clear sight of the hospital where Mum lay.

There was a plank of wood lying on the first step on the next flight of stairs up to the second floor, but the hospital showed clearly from up there. Wandering between the huge, open double doors on the south side of the main staircase, I could see across a vast room to a small tapestry-lined chamber, where an old man with a fringe of white hair around his bald pate sat snoozing in the sun.

He had a brown, dressing-gown-like garment draped around him. His feet were in a box of straw that covered his ankles, and his hands were folded across his stomach as he sat sleeping in a high-backed chair. As I stood watching, I suddenly realized that the reason Grace had not brought me upstairs in the morning was because some parts of the place were still occupied.

Thankful that the gentle-looking old man had not caught me trespassing, I slipped back to the main staircase and heard Billy calling. Looking over the bannister, I saw my white-faced brother and Grace standing in the great hall down below.

'Jo!' He sounded very anxious, 'Keep close to the wall and come down as lightly as you can.'

I did as he said, wondering why he was making so much fuss. All I had done was to try to keep the dog with me as I had been bidden. How was I to know that the whole fabric of the place was riddled with deathwatch beetle and dry rot, or that the main staircase had been considered too dangerous and unsafe to use for years.

'How does that old man in the brown cloak manage then?' I countered, but Billy said I was talking rubbish. I offered to go back up and ask the old chap to come down, but Grace said she knew all about him and that we must hurry back home.

Her parents had been worried enough when Bess had trotted home without me. What they would make of all this, heaven alone knew. Grace's father asked me a lot of questions, seeming extremely interested in the old man with his feet in the straw box. Although he seemed in no way angry, my clothes were collected back into the rush shopping bag they had arrived in. Billy and Grace then took me home.

Despite their reassurances that I had done nothing wrong, the feeling persisted that I had disgraced my brother and shamed my parents by intruding beyond some mysterious boundary, going where I was not supposed to go. I felt weepy and thoroughly dejected. Billy tried to explain that the home of Grace's mother and father was not really a suitable place for a child to stay, while the old mansion had proved to be very dangerous for the unwary to enter. Inside and out it was crumbling into decay.

I was back home again, but our old farmhouse did not seem like home at all. Here was a world of makeshift irregular meals, odd unwashed socks, unmade beds, unswept floors and atrocious attempts at part-time housekeeping by a bevy of older sisters, made short-tempered by their anxious concern for our sick mother and the fact that I was back home again, fidgeting, asking fool questions and generally getting under their feet.

I had not helped make life easier for anyone by having an attack of German measles. Time seemed to drag by on chained feet until the magic day when Dad brought Mum home from hospital. She looked limp and pale as a plant left forgotten and unwatered in a dark place, but gradually my little world swung back into the orbit of normality again.

Soon afterwards, the stately old mansion and all the parkland around was sold for redevelopment, Grace's family now being in the process of taking up the leasehold on a farm and moving from the lovely house that had for so long been their home.

Dad offered to lend them any farm implements that they might need but had not yet acquired, so Grace's father and mother drove over for an afternoon visit to express their thanks, bringing Grace with them. Such grown-up gatherings seemed boring, so I usually managed to creep away and find something more interesting to do. This time I was told to be on my best behaviour, proving to Grace's parents that I could behave properly by staying still and keeping my mouth shut.

'Remember, Jo. Seen but not heard, and no dashing off getting yourself grubby,' Mum had warned me.

Armed with a storybook, I sat on a stool between the red plush curtains and the window alcove. The waves of adult conversation flowed around me like the ripples of a calm sea lapping a shore. Grace's father was so kindly that I had at first believed him to be Father Christmas in disguise. On that afternoon, his distress was obvious as he spoke of the beautiful parkland and gardens being turned to mud and concrete, making new roads for the proposed vast housing estate.

Sharp of hearing as the little pig with the big ears, I took more notice when he said that the only spot left undisturbed and unflattened by the onslaught was the little chapel in the beech grove where nightingales always sang. Demolition contractors, already unsuccessfully attempting to knock down the mansion, intended to use explosives as the fastest, most economical and effective method of reducing it to rubble, their haste possibly aggravated by anxiety that there might well be public outcry at the destruction of an ancient building.

They had arranged for blasting operations to begin that afternoon. Rather than endure listening to the old place dying, Grace's father had chosen to visit us and discuss his farming future with our Dad.

'I don't know what the world is coming to,' he said sadly. 'I am thankful that Father Peter, who was priest-in-charge when his superiors eventually decided to close the place down as a college, is not around to witness what is happening today. The dear old chap tried so hard to prove that it could still survive as a viable proposition. He loved every stone and speck of soil around the place. He would work in the gardens keeping them tidy, although he must have been well past eighty when he died. The poor old man was so crippled up with circulation troubles and arthritis that he used to sit at his desk with his feet in a box of straw to keep them warm.'

Unthinking, my older sister Eve spoke up: 'Was he the man in a long brown cloak that Jo saw, then?'

A sensation of cold apprehension swept over me as I sat clutching the closed book between my quaking hands. Grace, who happened to be nearest to me, noticed the curtain trembling behind her chair. Taking it aside she grasped my hands.

'We don't want to sit here listening to a lot of talking do we, Jo? Suppose you take me and show me how to feed the chickens for your Mum.'

We went out into the sunshine of a spring afternoon, my beautiful grey-eyed future sister-in-law placing a comforting arm around my shoulder as she tried to explain that I had no cause to be afraid or anxious about something that was not at all unusual.

Everyone had a special perception, but most never used or even knew that they had it. Some could see much farther than others. Some could hear the sound of night-flying bats. There were those who could play music at a touch. I of all people should know that while most are right-handed, there were plenty of left-handed people about whose brains worked in a different way. There was absolutely nothing to fear.

As we fed the fowls and collected the eggs from the nest boxes, I remembered that I had seen a cackling old Rhode Island Red hen coming out of the garden shed. We delved among the flowerpots under the bench, with Grace bending her head to avoid the pungent bunches of dried herbs and skeins of onions hanging from the rafters.

As a series of rumbling explosions set the garden tools rattling on their wall rack, we knew that the old mansion had been blasted from the face of the earth. Grace stood statue still, her head bent, her arms around me. Her tears fell on my face as we stood with never a word spoken between us until she straightened up and set a skein of onions swinging.

Wiping her eyes, Grace said quietly, 'I'm like you, Jo. Onions make me cry.'

We picked up the basket and took the eggs we had collected to my Mum, who stood, wearing her best pinafore, by the kitchen door.

Among the Invited Guests

A pair of amorous doves had conducted incessant noisy rituals of courtship in the apple tree by the bedroom window since the first light of dawn. Their flutterings and continuous cooing exacerbated the discomfort of a night rendered sleepless for Florrie by an armoury of tight-wound metal curlers that were torturing her scalp.

Such vexations left her in no mood to allow her sleeping husband, Dick, to continue peacefully his imitation of an acorn-satiated hog snuffling and snorting beneath an oak tree.

Unmindful of the cottage-garden scent of early blooming wallflowers and violets, Florrie flounced out of bed, slamming the window on the dew-damp early-morning chill and the lovestruck pigeons, contriving to nudge Dick's back with an instantly awakening elbow on the way.

She dressed quickly, grumbling as she hid the hair-improving ironmongery beneath a mud-coloured headscarf, insisting on co-operation and the need for a two-hour-early start to the day.

Anyone could have believed that she had demanded that the world be set back a day by the fuss Dick had made about having their Saturday bath put forward to Friday, thus being a day early in changing his pants, shirt, socks and vest. Pointing a foot in the vague direction of his clean long-legged pants, sleep-hazy Dick privately pondered his conviction that the chap who first decided that women were the weaker sex had never met the likes of his Flo.

Breakfast time. Dick's first morning cup of tea was soured by Florrie's accusations that he had been intent on spoiling this special Easter Saturday ever since the expensive, deckle-edged, silver-printed invitation had arrived on that snowy January day. It was futile of him to argue that he could not alter his working routine, and that he could not begin his regular Saturday morning road-sweeping beat down through the village street until The Grange horse riders had passed through. No local crisis would arise if he swept his beat two hours early. In fact the garden lovers along the village street would gladly dash out with their fire shovels and pick up anything the horses dropped.

Florrie asked why was it that men acted so mule-headed when it came to wedding arrangements? The thought occurred to Dick this might be that they could not bear to see another poor fish being caught in the net of matrimony, but knowing that he always came a poor second in any battle of words with his wife, he said nothing, did as he was told, and left.

As soon as Dick had gone, Florrie wheeled his twenty-year-old Royal Enfield motorcycle and sidecar out of the shed. To emphasize to neighbours and other interested observers that her zealous polishing of the previous day had not been inspired by a measly, mundane, five-mile Saturday afternoon shopping jaunt, she tied a posy of lucky white heather with long white ribbon streamers to the stem of the side mirror.

Dick was home by eleven. After a quick wash and a cheese sandwich, he reluctantly submitted to the semi-strangulation of a new white shirt with a tight studded neckband anchoring a stiff starched collar. His blue serge suit had rarely left the camphor-ball-protected darkness of the clothes chest in the twenty-four years since he first bought it for his wedding. It was a tight fit.

He questioned the need to be dressed up like a dog's dinner when he could wear a perfectly good pair of grey flannels and his government surplus dispatch rider's leather jacket, helmet and goggles. Even Florrie must see that he could not ride along in a trilby hat, unless he used hatpins from the mantelpiece vase to anchor it on his head. Point conceded, Florrie agreed that she would carry the trilby hat until they were near to their destination, then he must stop and shed the goggles and helmet that made him look like a World War One aviator.

Relieved of the purgatorial curlers and chrysalis drabness of her workaday garb, Florrie emerged from the cottage as colourful as a tropical butterfly in the mauve, red, and yellow floral dress with matching jacket she had only finished sewing the previous evening. A home perm, stiff setting lotion, and her night of curler-tormented misery resulted in a satisfying bush of frizzy curls, topped by a quite remarkable wide-brimmed hat.

This designer creation would not have disgraced a duchess. Florrie had discovered it among the items collected from The Grange while she was sorting out goods for a white elephant stall at a village jumble sale. She had been astute enough to recognize that it had an elitist link with royalty, having been the Ascot hat worn by a wealthy race-horse-owning lady some years earlier. Photographs of her conversing with royalty in the paddock had featured in all the local newspapers at the time.

Quickly putting half-a-crown in the Oxo tin that was to serve as a cash box, Florrie put the hat aside and took it home to keep for unspecified future grand occasions. By the expensive look of the silver deckle-edged wedding invitation card, the special event was due to take place that day. Undoubtedly Florrie's Bond Street model hat had been seen in illustrious circles, but somehow the elegant ambience of Ascot was missing as she bustled out of the house. The wide-brimmed, exotic tropical-garden effect of the milliner's creation only served to give Florrie the appearance of an overweight pixie peering crossly from beneath a possibly poisonous toadstool.

It was no mean feat to retain any pretence of elegance while emulating the contortions of an overadventurous winkle anxiously retreating into the convolutions of its shell, but Florrie managed to ease her portly frame into the cramped confines of the sidecar. A blue tissue-wrapped wedding gift, a box of confetti and her umbrella left little space for her feet, nor was the situation eased by Dick attempting to jam his fiddle case down beside her as if she was a rattling window sash needing a wedge.

In the instant altercation, Dick uncharacteristically reminded his wife that given the chance, he would have been acting best man at Dan Backet's wedding, and later playing his fiddle for dancing at the reception in the village hall that day. If he had to go to the wedding of a niece he had not seen nor heard from for almost twenty years, he could at least offer to play his fiddle to liven up the proceedings. Scornfully, Florrie pointed out that a wedding reception held in a refined hotel was no place for the common 'jigging about' tunes he played.

As Dick encased her round with the celluloid windshield, canvas hood and side flaps of the sidecar, Florrie repeated her conviction that he should be taking his niece down the aisle today. After all, Dick was the only close blood relative the girl had. By rights he should be giving young Doreen away. It was not his fault, or Florrie's, that their offer to bring up his orphaned infant niece had been thrown back in their faces eighteen years before.

Florrie was never likely to forget or forgive that graveside scene with Dick still stunned that his young brother and sister-in-law had been killed on a level crossing, and that black-veiled, uppity, second cousin of Doreen's dead mother saying that her pompous-looking husband had already taken legal advice about taking over the child. Condescendingly this woman, Hilda, had explained.

'It is simply a matter of status, a question of which couple will be able to give the child a better life. Henry is highly regarded in the offices of the Gas Light and Coke Company, and destined for promotion. He belongs to several influential organizations. Your husband is a village road sweeper, I believe.'

All attempts to keep in touch with Dick's niece had been frozen out, with childhood birthday and Christmas postal orders grudgingly acknowledged, then nothing until this classy wedding invitation came out of the blue. Dick reluctantly agreed that maybe at so emotional a time as planning for her wedding, niece Doreen might feel the loss of her true parents and welcome his presence today.

Having acceded to Florrie's demand that he drive slowly

through the village to let her friends and neighbours see how smartly they were dressed for the occasion, Dick cruised along at a steady twenty miles an hour, savouring the almost unique experience of deliberately ignoring his nattering wife on the pretext of the engine noise of the Enfield making it impossible for him to hear.

This recalcitrant attitude and the jolting discomfort of her means of transport inevitably made Florrie's short-strung temper snap like overstretched elastic. Her bird-beak-shaped umbrella handle hooked into his shirt collar persuaded him that it might be wise to stop.

A volley of reproach was levelled at him as he drove onto the grass verge to ask what was wrong.

'Are you practising for a motorbike scramble, or taking us to your niece's posh wedding? If you had shoved a screw-topped jar of cream in beside your damned fiddle, it would have been churned up into butter by now. My insides are shook to a proper confusion. You're only riding like a maniac to upset my stomach so that we have to go home.'

Dick's denial died without drawing breath as Florrie carried on.

'You've always been antisocial, lacking in family feeling. I've worked hard to make us look as smart as the best of them, so now will you drive as if you want to take me to a wedding and are not trying to kill me off!'

Dick's unsuccessful attempt to get started again made him dismount. As that moment he discovered that the sidecar tyre was flat. He asked Florrie to reach for his tool roll and foot pump down beside her feet.

She had left them on the shed bench rather than risk spoiling her new outfit and shoes with the oily old things. It began to rain. The alternatives of Dick leaving Florrie with the sidecar while he went home for his repair kit, or to continue to the wedding with Florrie on the pillion, were both rejected.

Thoroughly disgruntled, Dick complained that it was no fault of his that they were stuck by the roadside instead of attending the wedding of someone who had not seen them from the time she was a child of three, and had ignored them ever since. If Florrie wanted to be part of a wedding celebration, there was Dan's 'do' in the village hall. The bride's father had already got two beer barrels set up, there would be hot pies by the dozen, and Dick had been asked if he would play his fiddle. What more did Florrie want?

'It's not a case of wanting,' Florrie said tartly, 'I had hoped that for once in our lives we would think on a higher plane than hot meat pies, and mix with a better class of people.'

The state of impasse was eventually resolved by an AA patrol man, who stopped his yellow motorcycle and side car, expressing his admiration for Dick's old Royal Enfield bike. His question of Dick's breakdown services membership provoked a somewhat bedraggled Florrie into retorting that until this day of his only relative's wedding, her husband never usually reckoned to venture beyond the distance that he could wheel the bike home.

Dick's explanation about the missing tool roll prompted the remark, 'I'm married too, mate! Have this puncture repair on me.'

Behind time, and hampered by an increasing amount of city-bound Easter traffic, Florrie attempted to direct Dick through unfamiliar streets from a route map of a prewar city carnival programme. She did well until they were caught up in the one-way system that was not on the map at all. Thoroughly flustered, remembering that she had left their invitation card at home, and suddenly aware that they were going round in circles, Florrie saw a street sign with a name that seemed familiar.

Amid some fist shaking from other road users, Dick made a sharp right turn. Uncertainty turned to relief when they saw beribboned cars parked outside a church, and a photographer adjusting his tripod on the path. As they approached, he asked them to stand aside because the 'Wedding March' was playing, so the bridge and groom would be coming out.

There were swarms of well-dressed guests, many of the men in 'tails and toppers'. Florrie confessed she would not have recognized Hilda and Henry, and Doreen certainly did not favour Dick's family when it came to looks. Money was obviously no object. Dick was all for retreating behind the gravestones, but they were rounded up for the group photographs, and thankfully followed the line of limousines to a prestigious hotel. The doorman gave Dick an odd look as he parked the motorbike.

There was such a crush around the bride and groom, Florrie could only hand the wedding gift to the flustered-looking girl, introduce themselves, and move on.

Avoiding the crowded foyer, Florrie led Dick through some glass doors, beyond which the wedding breakfast tables were set out. Her inability to find their name cards was overcome by simply removing two 'And Partner' cards and shuffling a few others about a bit.

Some displaced guests caused confusion at their table until Florrie struck up a conversation with a frightfully upper-crust middle-aged lady dressed in a plain navy and white linen suit, considered by Florrie to be extremely drab as a wedding outfit. An Ascot hat like hers that had bowed to royalty could outclass any others there. The woman, questioning their right to be there, needed to be put in her place.

'By rights we should be sitting at the top table,' Florrie began huffily. 'Dick is the bride's only living relative on her real father's side, even if she was adopted when she was three.'

'Is that so? How very interesting!' The lady turned to another guest in a rare state of excitement.

'My dear! You will never guess at the cuckoo that has just flown out of the bridal family tree. I can't wait to see Jeremy's parents' faces when I tell them that their new daughter-in-law is not what they imagine. Her father was once a Gas Works clerk.'

Dick nudged Florrie to keep quiet. She had to admit that as wedding breakfasts went, this reception was in a class of its own.

The first uneasy intimation that all was not as it seemed came when the speeches and the toasts began. The best man raised his glass.

'To know Fiona and Jeremy is to love them.' Dick and Florrie looked at each other with reddening faces, aware that they did not know the young couple at all.

'Strewth, Flo! We're at the wrong wedding,' Dick whispered. 'Let's get out of here. Pretend to feel faint or something.'

'There's not much pretence, I can tell you!' Florrie retorted indignantly. 'Fancy getting us in here under false pretences. They've brought me out in a hot flush! I'm taking our present back too, if I can manage it on the way out.'

With his wife once again installed in the sidecar, complete with the blue tissue-wrapped wedding gift, Dick asked wearily, 'Where now then? Maybe our best bet is to cruise round until we can see a road sign showing us a way of of the city, and then head home.'

Completely lost, and passing through increasingly shabby areas while still trying to find their bearings, Florrie recognized the name of the street she now remembered as being on the wedding invitation. On the corner was the church dedicated to the correct saint. As Dick drove slowly along, he noticed several white beribboned cars in the parking lot of a shabby hotel that looked more like a noisy back-street pub.

'That's it!' Florrie shouted triumphantly. 'Doreen's wedding reception is being held at The Crown Hotel.'

Dick parked the bike, Florrie insisting that their wedding gift stay hidden with Dick's fiddle and her umbrella beneath the canvas cover of the sidecar until they had definitely established that mischance had not brought them to the wrong wedding twice in one day. The indignity of having to retrieve their present from a stack of others on display was not an experience Florrie would wish to endure again.

Adjusting her hat to a no-nonsense angle, and straightening the artificial chrysanthemum in Dick's buttonhole as if defying it to droop, Florrie purposefully led the way to the front entrance porch of the hotel. This opened straight into a tatty-looking bar.

A plump, over-made-up, middle-aged woman, with a curled heap of unlikely-looking ginger hair piled on top of her head, paused from arranging jars of cockles and jellied eels along the shelf behind the bar. Ignoring Florrie, she beamed suggestively to Dick.

'What would you like me to get for you then, my love?'

Dick being unused to such offers, could only stand goggling as she leaned across the counter, exposing a prodigious amount of wobbling cleavage that appeared to be trying to escape from the confines of an overtight, low-fronted, leopard-spot-patterned satin blouse.

A wifely dig in the ribs brought Dick back from the realms of erotic fantasy. Florrie certainly knew how to cut a chap down to size.

'He's not your love, and he's not buying anything you have to offer. Heaven knows you've got your wares set out in your shop window plain for all to see. I suppose you can't help being top heavy and deformed. A good strong boned bust bodice would help to stop you looking as if you're walking around with a couple of pink blancmanges that have been turned out of their moulds before they were properly set. Where is the wedding reception being held then? We are important guests who have been delayed.'

'Important! That lot?' the visibly reddening barmaid nodded to a door marked 'Private' at the rear of the bar, adding a begrudged: 'Through there.'

Lit by a solitary unshaded, low-wattage bulb, the airless dark-green-painted passageway beyond the doorway reeked of stale beer, cabbage water, cigarette smoke, disinfectant and something far less pleasant.

The sound of shouting and loud music increased in intensity as they came to a large, hot, overcrowded room at the back. The place heaved with young couples gyrating to a record player turned to full volume. They stood together, momentarily hesitant, but they had been seen by the thoroughly flustered-looking mother of the bride.

'It's called The Twist,' Hilda said, nodding towards the dancers as she confessed she hardly knew any of Doreen's friends. 'I think there are a lot of gate-crashers. They've descended like a plague of locusts, eating and drinking the place dry. I hope they don't turn nasty when they find out they will have to pay for any other booze they want. Of course, our Doreen has married beneath her. Two of Kirk's uncles got fighting and most of his lot have gone home. I'll let Doreen know you are here, and Henry will get you a sherry from the bottle we've kept hidden.'

Florrie instantly recognized the now bald-headed Henry. He was dealing with a young man who was being violently sick.

There was a lull in the music. Doreen, a bulging rather than blushing bride, was far more interested in getting her new, but extremely inebriated husband on his feet, than in welcoming long-lost relatives. Glaring in Florrie and Dick's direction, fully aware that they could hear her, she upbraided Hilda for having ever invited the obviously unwelcome guests.

'What's it to me if the weird-looking pair of old turnip-crunchers are my aunt and uncle? I didn't want to invite them in the first place. Don't let on that they are my relatives. Kirk and his gang would laugh their heads off and I would never live it down.'

At that moment a barman, passing with mop and bucket, called Dick aside.

'If that is your old motorbike and sidecar outside, mate, I'd keep a sharp eye on it. There are them around here who will have it stripped down to its wheel marks as soon as it gets dark.'

Dick looked anxiously at his wife, who needed no persuading to take her leave, but Florrie, being Florrie, was determined to say her piece.

Very purposefully, loud and clear, she bade farewell to the bride, her beer-logged husband and everyone else.

'Hilda and Henry must have paid more money than they have got sense to put on this reception. It is a pity the wedding was not arranged for a month's time. Doreen and that drunken sponge could have celebrated a christening at the same time. I am proud to say that I am not related to anyone here, nor from this moment is my husband. In bringing up Doreen as they have, Hilda and Henry deserve all they have got. Dick may never have amounted to more than a council roadman, but we are respectable and respected people. This is no place for such as us. Come along, Dick. We are going home.'

Their journey home was uneventful, Florrie keeping remarkably calm and quiet. Dick slowed down, stopping as they approached the village hall. He suggested they call in to offer Dan and his bride their good wishes. Somewhat reluctantly, Florrie complied.

Taking Dick's fiddle and the now rather battered blue tissue-wrapped wedding gift with them, they went into the hall, somewhat overwhelmed by the welcome awaiting them. Minus his collar and tie, the father of the bride came forward.

'Come on, Dick! Let your neck out of prison and give us a couple of lively tunes to start the dancing. There's a barrel just been broached and Florrie looks as if she could do with a nice cup of tea.'

'I expect this seems a bit countryfied and tame after the wedding you've been to,' Dan's Mum remarked as they stood in the kitchen making a special pot of tea.

'That was a family obligation, but we wanted to get back and give Dan and Ada another little present.' In handing over the much-travelled gift, the tissue wrapping parted company to reveal a glass celery vase. Helping to rewrap it, Dan's Mum remarked that her old aunt used to have one similar to it before she died and they had sent everything the house-clearers would not take to a jumble sale. Pouring out the tea, she said she supposed that Florrie had been drinking champagne. Florrie shook her head.

'Champagne drinking is an overrated pastime, tasting no different to fizzy fruit salts as far as I'm concerned. Dick's work makes him no lover of weddings. As a road sweeper he knows that when they are over there is little left but wet confetti and regrets. Now, will you shut the door and stand guard while I slacken off the laces of my new corset and take off my posh hat?'

'That's a rare sort of hat, Florrie, not the kind you'd get from the Bon Marche for half-a-crown.'

'No, you wouldn't,' Florrie answered conspiratorially as they drank the tea. 'I will let you into a secret, seeing I'll not be wearing it again. It came from The Grange. Lady Muck wore it to Ascot the year two of their horses ran there. This hat has bobbed to the Queen and probably graced all sorts of other aristocratic occasions, but you will never believe the places it has been today.'

A rare sense of contentment descended over Florrie as Dan's Mum suggested they went and found themselves two large glasses of port and lemon.

Dick was busy playing, fiddling away in his short sleeves. Florrie smiled at him in passing as she followed the bridegroom's mother out into the hall.

Prompt Settlement Will Oblige

Anyone witnessing my bustling country mother's marathon market-day shopping expeditions could understand why my five older sisters resorted to all manner of excuses to avoid having to assist on this muscle-bulging endurance test.

Being the youngest, with least to say in the matter, I was frequently selected as her companion. Any attempt to argue was swiftly overcome by Mum's particular brand of logic and reason. I had two hands capable of holding shopping basket handles, and since I was still of an age to travel at half adult fare for the five-mile journey of our country bus route, that was a fourpenny bonus for a start. With our finances verging from not too good to downright sickly, Mum was an inveterate seeker-out of bargains, happily humping home the heaviest household necessities if they were a halfpenny cheaper than the price charged by our village shop. Like a small skiff tied to a bustling, steam-powered tug-boat, I bobbed through the streets and around the market stalls behind her.

Hampered and encumbered by deep, overladen, woven-rush shopping bags, I was forever apologizing to pedestrians I barged into while trying to stay in sight of the pink and purple artificial peonies adorning my mother's second-best Sunday hat.

By the time her purchasing power was spent and we were waiting for the bus that would take us within a mile of our home, these flowers seemed to droop visibly, or maybe it was just that the lethal, glass-jewelled hatpins that anchored her hat, and the hedge-stake hairpins beneath it, had failed to keep her topknot bun of hair secure, allowing it to subside in straggling wisps all around her neck.

On one particular April shopping trip, when the prospect of various relatives arriving for a cost-free country Easter drove Mum to some keen purse searching and even keener bargain hunting, we seemed to complete our shopping tour without the usual strain and rush. With at least ten minutes to spare by the almost infallible Corn Exchange Hall clock, we stood by the market square watching for the Flying Dutchman's bus.

Making the most of the waiting time to check through all the shopping bags in case there was anything she had forgotten, Mum found an important letter she had omitted to post. Miss Forsdyke Ashington Smythe, a wealthy pillar of the upper, more impeccable, local social strata, had owed Dad fifty pounds in respect of horse fodder, et cetera, for so long the he had penned this latest reminder in red ink, printing 'Prompt settlement will oblige' in large letters by her address on the envelope. There was no time to post it in the city, so Mum decided we would pop it into the post office pillar box when the bus disgorged us in our own village street.

We stood around aimlessly watching the market-day world go by and heard three-quarter-hour chimes from the Corn Exchange clock. Mum became so increasingly agitated that the old hurdy-gurdy man failed to evoke her usual toe-tapping response to his cheerful music. Somewhat concerned that she looked so anxious, he volunteered to stand guard over all her laden shopping bags and baskets cluttering the footpath, while Mum and I went to enquire of various pavement stall holders if they had seen the Flying Dutchman or his bus.

'Been gone about two hours, I reckon,' was the lugubrious response of one trader. Mum's face was a study of disbelief and dismay.

'But we were waiting long before his bus was due to leave at half-past one,' she contended. 'Even now it is only ten past two by the Corn Exchange clock.'

Back came the irritable answer: 'Don't blame me if you're an hour adrift in your timing, missus! They ain't got around to altering the clock forward to summertime yet, the dozy devils, or maybe they are like a lot of others, not keen to mess about with nature altering dark and sunrise with "Daylight Saving Time".'

The next scheduled bus service run to our village was due to leave the city in two and a half days' time. To me the prospect of the long trudge home seemed extremely daunting, but Mum set her hat straight, squared her shoulders and said that it was a lovely afternoon for having a two-hour stroll home. She persuaded the hurdy-gurdy man that a chestnut post had outlived the purpose for which it was intended, the rose bush it supported by the market entrance horse trough being definitely dead.

The post was pushed through the handles of the shopping bags and baskets so that we could carry them between us, a ploy I would recommend to no one along the crowded pavements and narrow streets of a busy town on market day. While some of the baskets swung sedately as we walked, there were those that seemed intent to shed their contents.

My Mum's culinary skill of turning economy-priced offal into tasty meals for her family meant that she bought such bargains on her market-day shopping forays. There were few occupations more ignoble than scooping up innumerable pig's trotters and a bullock's heart that had slipped through their blood-stained newspaper wrappings to scatter among the feet of passing pedestrians in a busy street.

We plodded on, thankful to be approaching quieter suburbs with less crowded pavements. Our hopes for a lift blossomed as we saw a familiar vehicle pass by, slowing down to stop a few hundred yards ahead.

'Quick, Jo! Run fast as you can and try to stop Short Foot Price. It's the day for his village round, so ask him nicely if he will oblige us with a lift home in his drapery van.'

Short Foot, the travelling draper – so named because he had

been known to give short measure when it came to yards, feet and inches – was an obsequious, unctuous little man. We found him trying to placate an irate customer who had purchased some stockings from his van, only to find that they scarcely reached her knees.

'Of course, madam, you are blessed with beautifully long limbs, if you will forgive mentioning the matter,' Short Foot said smartly, by which time my mother had most of our shopping bags firmly entrenched among his wares.

'Graceful as a swan, madam, no offence or personal comment intended,' Short Foot continued. The plump middle-aged person smiled happily, admitted she had been somewhat hasty, and agreed that she could use the offending stockings as an Easter gift to a relative she did not particularly like.

'But, Mum, a swan's got short waddling legs,' I whispered, receiving an elbow in the ribs by way of reply.

With Mum safely ensconced in the passenger seat, and myself perched in among the cards of elastic, laces, combinations and tea towels, I sat with the suspenders from an assorted bundle of steel-boned, fearsome-looking, salmon-pink corsets dangling around my face. Short Foot chattered as he drove.

'I suppose you have been buying a new Easter frock for your daughter? Paying dearly too, dear lady, if you buy from the city shops. Seeing you are a cash customer, I could offer you a cheap garment ideal for an in-between, odd-sized sort of child.'

My patently honest mother admitted that the present family finances would not allow such purchases, and she had no intention of getting into debt.

'Money!' Short Foot sighed. 'Dear lady, I stay poor through other people's debts.'

That reminded Mum of her unposted bill for Miss Forsdyke Ashington Smythe. Since Short Foot's round would not take him in the vicinity of our farm until tea time, he agreed to set us down at the top of Lockley Hill, within about two hundred yards of that illustrious person's driveway gate.

Mum decided to deliver the bill herself, thus saving a penny stamp. Still lugging our shopping bags, we walked along the crunching gravel drive to deposit them on the white-stoned front steps. Ethel Pearce, Miss Forsdyke Ashington Smythe's fourteen-year-old maid, and my erstwhile school friend, answered the door bell.

'Madam is "At Home" this afternoon,' she told us, a wry expression flitting across her face. 'Best let me put your shopping in the cloakroom before I show you into the drawing room with them other posh old girls.'

Lightened of our load, we followed Ethel along a carpet-covered corridor and into a plush-curtained, over-upholstered, fussy-looking room. Three other ladies were present, watching the lady of the household filling elegant cups with tea. She looked somewhat surprised as Ethel announced us, but invited us to sit down, and handed round a cake stand of dainty, one-bite sandwiches. I wished Mum had been able to tidy the hair that hung down beneath her hat and was suddenly conscious of my concertina-wrinkled stockings and scuffed boots.

'How quaintly charming,' said our hostess. 'To what do we owe this pleasure?' I watched her cronies smirk.

All dignity, Mum drew the red-ink-written bill from her coat pocket and answered, 'Actually, madam, I have called on you seeking immediate settlement of this. Fifty pounds may count as little to folk of your standing and social position. To a struggling farmer like my husband, it is so vital that I have decided to sit here until you settle at least a substantial portion of your debt.'

There was an air of shocked silence for a moment, after which Mum conversed with the other ladies about the weather and the late arrival of spring. Our hostess swept out of the room, holding the offending bill as if it had fallen into something nasty. She returned, tugged a fireside bell pull to summon Ethel, then handed Mum an envelope with banknotes inside it. These Mum promptly counted, offering to sign the bill by way of receipt.

Ethel hovered in the doorway. Miss Forsdyke Ashington Smythe issued her instructions.

'Show this woman out, Ethel. And by the tradesman's entrance, if you please.'

'That was one in the eye for old Snooty,' Ethel said gleefully as she reunited us with our shopping bags.

We reached home just before Short Foot's van drew up in the farmyard.

'If it is good value, I could afford to get young Jo that frock you offered at a reduced price,' Mum conceded. Short Foot cheerfully fetched it from his van.

It was light blue with purple and yellow stripes, shapeless as a football jersey, fitting where it touched and sagging well below my knees. Mum doubted that the purple stripes would be colour fast, and was convinced that something of better value could be found in the city stalls and shops for the five shillings and eleven-pence three farthings it would cost. If I went with her on her next shopping expedition, she could probably hunt down a reasonably priced Easter frock.

Faced with this dread prospect as the alternative to Short Foot's special offer, I grasped the wretched baggy garment as if I admired every shapeless yellow and purple fold.

Making appropriate noises of excited appreciation, I told Mum that this fashionable style was just what I wanted.

'Are you sure?' Mum answered uncertainly, never knowing how I prayed for a bitterly cold Easter, thus giving me an excuse to hide the awfulness of Short Foot's bargain-offer frock under a long cardigan or my old winter coat.

A Touch of the Jaunders

There were all the orders for Christmas poultry to be dealt
with during the day, but I was determined not to waste
the two shillings I had invested in a lucky number ticket
to the annual Grand Christmas Social being held in our village
hall that night.

With aching arms, and lungs that felt as if they were lined
with duck down, Mum and I persevered with the unpleasant task
of preparing the birds for the table, until a row of naked-looking
cockerels, two fat geese, and four oven-ready ducks were lined up
along the stone slab dairy shelf.

By the time the last feathers had been swept away and the
place scrubbed down, I was left with about an hour in which to
get ready for my evening out, but first I had to wash the all-
pervading smell of poultry from my hair.

Normally I was content to use soft soap and rain water to wash my long mouse-coloured tresses. My father used to maintain that a woman's hair was her crowning glory, but even he had to acknowledge the fact that mine was soft, slippery, self-willed, and straight as a sick pig's tail.

My hair shed grips like autumn leaves, but that night I was determined to attempt a transformation, having spent fourpence on a Curly Girl shampoo. Perhaps I should have paid less attention to the query, 'Do you want billowing curls that gleam with colour?' and more to the small print advising that 'This powder must be mixed in a glass or china vessel! Use no metal jugs!'

Having no time to dither, I carted jugs of warm water out to the two enamel washbowls in the scullery, and poured the shampoo mixture over my head. It made my eyes smart, so feeling, rather than seeing what I was doing, I washed my hair and rough towelled it dry.

Peering anxiously into the damp-speckled mirror by lamplight, my hair appeared to be no different. All I had for fourpence was a khaki-streaked face and neck, and a pair of ginger-tinted hands. Nothing seemed to shift the stains. Assisted by Mum, I tried salt, scouring powder, and a paste of oatmeal and egg whites. Even lemon juice failed to tone it down.

With a remnant of ruby-red velvet and a free dress pattern, I had sewn myself a pretty Christmassy dress, trimmed with a cream lace collar. I doubted if it would tone in with the colours of my hands and face.

'Stick some of that rubbishy old face powder on to hide it,' Mum suggested, remembering another 'brilliant idea' I had almost been tempted to waste my money on. 'Poudre Tokay' was supposed to attract every rich prince and potentate within a mile radius of the wearer. The box I sent for as a free sample brought me out in spots.

Nevertheless spots were preferable to looking the same colour as a sick camel and, as Mum said, I could hide my hands by being really ladylike and wearing gloves. The pity was that the only pair I had that were presentable were the ones Mum had made from an old leather coat, and lined with rabbit fur.

Everyone reckoned to contribute something to the Christmas Social, the only stipulation being that no beer, spirits or alcoholic beverages were permissible in the hall.

Our contribution was some of Mum's home-made ginger beer,

lemonade, and black cherry cordial to enliven the customary bowls of fruit cup punch. Late, and in a rush to leave, I collected a dozen bottles from the dark, stone-floored cupboard, put them in a basket and lashed that on the carrier of my old bike. Bottles rattling, hoping that the mud and puddles would not ruin my high-heeled shoes and new silk stockings, I rode along the dark and lonely lane, my still-damp hair clinging clammy to my neck. The chill wind whistled past my 'pearl', pear-drop earrings and gave me pins and needles in my ears.

'My saints, girl! You'm not sickening for the jaunders, are you?' Albert Parsley, acting doorkeeper, enquired, deeply concerned for the colour of my face. Blushing scarlet under the khaki, I crept into the hall kitchen where the refreshments were being set out and sampled by best-frocked ladies in satin pinnies. I volunteered to help Mrs Pearce mix up the fruit cup punch, chopping fruit, and dropping it into a huge earthenware bread crock, adding various bottles of fruit cordial and stirring it around.

'Why don't you go in along with the other young folk, Jo?' Mrs Grommet enquired, doling out jelly from a bucket as I inadvertently stepped back into a tray of trifles that were on the floor.

'Do 'ee let her bide now, Ethel,' said Mrs Pearce protectively. 'Can't you see the poor girl is far from well?'

The consensus of opinion was that after we had added all the fizzy stuff and tasted it to see if it was drinkable, it would be time to get some of the menfolk to carry the bread crock out into the hall. Thankful that the focus of attention had moved away from my ginger hands and blotchy features, I took the bottles from my basket and poured some of the contents in.

'I always say there is no one like your mother when it comes to getting a sparkle into lemonade, and the colour of the cherry cordial really helps.' Mrs Pearce, tasting by the teacupful, thought it was the best punch she had ever mixed. The other ladies sampling confirmed this opinion.

By the time they were finished, it needed four more bottles of lemonade and one of cherry cordial to top up the bread crock. I had a couple of sips of the punch. Two separate reasons made me pick up my cup and the empties and take them to the cupboard-like storeroom just outside the kitchen door. Firstly, I realized that the bottles I had collected so haphazardly contained not lemonade but parsley champagne. True, the others did have 'Cherry' written on the label, but it was not cordial I had brought along and tipped so blithely into the fruit cup.

Three bottles of home-made, five-year-old cherry ale had been stirred into the bread crock. I could only hide the bottles and hope for the best. Whatever effect it was to have on anyone else, the fruit punch had made my evening already, even if I did not drink it. In doling out the other helpers' 'tasters', I had spilled some, and noticed that the liquid took the ginger stain from off the back of my hand.

Carefully conserving the precious liquid, I scrubbed my face, neck and hands. It ruined my hanky, but worked wonders for my skin.

'Feeling better now, love?' Mrs Pearce asked as I went back to attempt to dilute our 'fruit' drink. I said I would be fine once I could just wash my hands and face.

'You look a different girl now,' the motherly soul continued. Off you go out there and join in the fun.'

A game of postman's knock was in progress, with much giggling and harmless pecking, until Billy Belton said that, given the choice, he would rather be kissed by his old nanny goat than by big Bertha. So far as postman's knock was concerned, his opinion was that she rated the same value as a wrongly addressed postcard that had lost its stamp.

We danced a Sir Roger de Coverley and a Paul Jones, followed by the Valeta. Then a few of the more avant-garde started dancing the new-fangled rumba, until the gramophone broke down.

More refreshments and more fruit punch were consumed, everyone agreeing that all this jollification gave one a powerful thirst.

To the musical accompaniment of Miss Minnie, the village organist, rendering 'The Maiden's Prayer', and 'Over The Waves' on an out-of-tune piano with four notes gone, we played musical chairs, but this deteriorated into musical laps, which some considered to be 'going a bit too far'.

'Do you know that when the lamplight catches your hair, it has an almost green and copper-coloured sheen?' said the blacksmith's eldest son as we sat out the next couple of games.

A few solos were sung and a game where anyone paying a forfeit had to don an article of clothing drawn from a hopsack with a walking stick. Parading around in jangling suspendered whale-boned corsets, voluminous bloomers, nightshirts, combinations and a variety of headgear, seemed to loosen inhibitions quite amazingly.

Then a game of pass the orange was played. This entailed tucking the orange under one's chin and passing it to one's neighbour without using the hands. It went fine until tiny Miss Minnie tried to pass it on to tall Bobby Button. In the process, the orange slid down the front of Miss Minnie's blouse and lodged around her waist.

'No hands, mind!' yelled the opposition.

Blushing as Bobby's face descended to the level of her midriff, Miss Minnie said primly, 'Mr Button, do desist!'

Undoing the button of her skirt, Bobby said, 'Joggle up and down a bit there, missus!' Of such initiative are battles, games, and fair hearts won!

I collected the three lucky number entrance tickets from my coat pocket when the draw for the prizes started. Mum and Dad always bought one each although they never came. Each ticket won a prize. It seemed a cheek to claim them until I saw what we had won. A bottle of raspberry vinegar, a battered box containing two cigars and bearing the inscription 'Happy Birthday from Mother' – all this and an old boiling hen, unplucked and freshly killed.

I had plucked enough chickens to last until next Christmas, and the other two items were of no account.

I would have loved to have seen Miss Minnie's face when she found the chicken hanging on her door latch. Bobby Button too, must have wondered about his gift, with the wording amended from 'Mother' to 'Minnie' – but such mysteries were all part of our country life.

The Bed Warmers

Having shepherded five younger brothers and sisters safely back from school, thirteen-year-old Louisa dodged beneath the lines of limp wet washing hung out across the sunless entry and sat playing five stones on the doorstep of her city tenement home. Her mother greeted her with unusual animation.

'Louey, come in here. You can tell that uppity school ma'am you'll be leaving come Friday. I'm a poor deserted creature, and you have reached Standard Seven, so she can't argue. Mr Rudd, who delivers milk to Widow Weeks, wants a living-in maid, so she put in a good word. You can start work for him on Saturday. Ain't you a lucky girl?'

Louisa's mind raced with unanswered questions, but her mother's grasp of the situation seemed remote. All she could find out was that the milkman lived in the country and she must be ready to leave with him when he came on his Saturday round. Every spare minute of the next few days was spent in helping Widow Weeks patch and make over second-hand clothes to put in a borrowed wickerwork box.

It was from Widow Weeks that Louisa learned of the arrangement that the milkman would take half-a-crown to her mother every Saturday, plus buttermilk left over from churning twice a week. Louisa was to be given sixpence to spend just how she pleased. On the following Saturday morning, Louisa spent hours watching for the grey pony and milk float in the street. Then suddenly it was outside Widow Weeks's place. An elderly man with piercing light blue eyes and a mop of light-coloured, curly hair poking out around the brim of his brown bowler hat, looked her up and down. He called to Widow Weeks.

'I likes a maid to look plump and contented as a little pigeon, but this little scraggy thing looks as white as my smock. If she be a whiner, I promise you, missus, she'll be back tomorrow morning with the milk. Set your hamper down between the churns then, maid, for I ain't got all day.'

Cramped, cold, and exceedingly apprehensive, Louisa perched on the chariot-like vehicle, too shy and tongue-tied to speak as her employer continued his round.

The pony seemed to know where to stop without being guided. Time and again, her new employer went into customers' houses with his oval-lidded pail. He lingered to have a long and earnest discussion with a scruffy man on a street corner, but eventually they left the city behind them and were driving through country lanes. All her life Louisa had dreamed of going into the country, but now she was too cold and frightened to enjoy the ride.

Her new employer glared at her, saying, 'Be you feared or something? You have no need to be, for I'll not harm 'ee. A few puddens under your weskit and you'll be right as ninepence.'

They passed along a village street where a group of women, gossiping in a gateway, smirked and called: 'Morning, Mus' Rudd,' staring at Louisa as if she was something that had fallen from the sky.

At the end of a hoof-churned track, amid a cluster of wooden outbuildings, was a large lapwood-fronted dwelling. Mr Rudd drove the pony into a muddy paved yard.

'Take yourself indoors, girl, and get busy,' he ordered.

Hesitantly Louisa carried her clothes hamper towards the open back door of the house. A girl, somewhat older and plumper than herself, came running to answer her tugging at the bell pull on the wall.

'Please, Mr Rudd says I'm to help the missus here,' Louisa explained.

'There's no missus here except for Miss Millie, and she's the housekeeper,' the girl retorted.

'Ella! Don't stand gossiping at the door, girl!' a woman's deep voice called from within.

The girl answered, 'I ain't, Miss Millie. Some scrawny kid here says she's been set on to work!'

The unseen voice materialized into a tall, buxom woman, darkly dressed, but with flouncing petticoats rustling underneath.

'Where did Mr Rudd find you then? Put your clothes box down, child. No one wants to steal it. You look too puny for dairy work.'

In one lingering attempt to establish her own personal rights, Louisa retorted that she was wiry, not puny. If Mr Rudd's friend Widow Weeks had known she would get this sort of reception, she would expect her to be back on her doorstep with the milk the following day.

'Who is this Widow Weeks then?' the housekeeper asked, instructing Louisa in the art of scalding out dirty milk churns. 'Come along, Ella – and you too, girl. The cows are coming in.'

'What now?' Louisa wondered aloud.

Ella mimicking her, retorted: 'What now, you ninny? There are fifteen cows to milk, of course.'

'I can't milk cows,' Louisa stuttered.

Miss Millie, overhearing, said sharply, 'Then you had better soon learn!'

'Don't pay too much heed to her,' Ella whispered. 'Her bark be worse than her bite. She be a bit riled about your widow lady. Jim the herdsman and me will see you right.'

They put her stool down beside a placid old shorthorn, but her fingers grew numb with trying, and no milk went into the pail.

Then she saw her employer standing beside her.

'She'll not let her milk down with you tugging away, child. Coax her gently and she'll co-operate. Females are all the same.'

The next few hours flew by in a turmoil of hard work and instructions, then the kitchen table was set for the evening meal. Louisa had never seen so much food, even at Christmas. Mr Rudd and Miss Millie sat in tall-backed chairs on either side of the fireplace while the two girls cleared away. By the time this was finished, Ella had explained why their employer needed to go to the city slums to find a new dairymaid.

His doubtful marital status and his reputation with women made the local mothers determined that their daughters give him and his jobs a wide berth. He had only lived in the place for fifteen years, so was still a comparative stranger.

'He's got his hands too full to bother the likes of you and me beyond a quick peck and a pinch,' Ella continued. 'But you really put the ferret among the tame rabbits when you mentioned his widow lady friend.'

Louisa said that Mr Rudd lingered just as long at other customers' homes, and talked to tramps on street corners. It was silly to cast aspersions. Ella, looking worldly-wise, told her that their employer often backed horses with a bookie's runner, and that rumour accredited him with a dozen unofficial offspring on his rounds.

Soon after they returned to the kitchen, Miss Millie asked, 'Will you have cocoa tonight, or your special nightcap, Mr Rudd.

'The nightcap, I fancy,' her employer said staidly.

Louisa was initiated into the art of whisking brandy, salt and pepper into two raw eggs. As the mantel clock chimed the half-hour after eight, Miss Millie ordered the two girls upstairs to bed. By candlelight Ella led Louisa up a winding, uncarpeted staircase, lifting the string latch of a door on the landing. Inside, on an island of rugs surrounded by a vast expanse of lino, stood an iron bedstead, huge and wide. Louisa could hardly believe she was to sleep in such palatial surroundings.

'Is this where we really sleep, Ella?' she said doubtfully as she donned her nightgown.

'Course not!' the older girl retorted. 'Mr Rudd can't abide getting between cold sheets, so us maids are sent up half an hour early every night to warm his bed.'

The few evasive maternal warnings flared like beacon fires in Louisa's mind: 'I'm not getting into some dirty old man's bed,' she insisted.

'Daft ha'p'orth! All we do is scuttle up to the attic with our things as he opens that door from the side room where he undresses. As we hop out of bed, he hops in.'

Louisa still had doubts, but climbed into the soft feather bed. For all that she was dog-tired, she sat up talking. Ella told her that the wardrobe was full of women's clothes. Among them was a fox fur tippet that Miss Millie hankered after, but Mr Rudd would not entertain any such show of affection, much less marriage. In Ella's opinion, he found life more comfortable as it was. Louisa had imagined the two to be barely on polite terms with each other.

Full of the wisdom of her sixteen summers, Ella enlightened her about the 'cocoa or nightcap' ritual. 'When he has that, she will be keeping him warm soon after we go up to the attic. But they still call each other Mr Rudd and Miss Millie even when they are tucked up together in bed.'

So began the pattern of Louisa's days and nights. The two girls took a keen interest in Miss Millie's outwardly prim attempts to become their employer's wife. He often came home less than sober. Then came the day when his drink-addled mind had some vague memory of putting the weekly takings on a treble horse-racing bet. This was confirmed next day when he returned, doling out pound notes and saying he was suddenly absurdly rich.

He draped the fox fur tippet around Miss Millie's shoulders and gave her a ruby ring. She was never to become Mrs Rudd, for the dairyman was found dead on his rounds. With a dairy herd to tend, Miss Millie made all the decisions and arrangements until they followed him to his grave. There, in company with Mr Rudd's legal adviser, stood a woman in deep mourning.

She approached Miss Millie, Ella and Louisa.

'So you three were his harem. Well, I own everything now. You can have a fortnight's pay and be gone by tomorrow night. I'll have my fur back too,' she concluded, yanking the fox fur tippet from around Miss Millie's neck.

When Louisa arrived home to the sunless court the next morning, she found that a new baby had arrived while she had been away. Her new brother had light blue eyes, a mop of light curly hair, and a familiar look about him somehow.

'What a terrible waste and a shame about Mr Rudd,' her mother said by way of greeting. 'Being a poor deserted woman, I shall miss him calling. He was such a lovely man.'

Johnny Goes A-Maying

River mist rose wraithlike from the water after sunset, enfolding the silent streets. Night in the city found the low-lying courts and alleys shrouded in sooty, self-perpetuating fog made foul with the rancid stench of the tallow-boiling tanks of the soap works and the reeking hide-steeping vats in the adjoining tannery yard.

A terrace of five mean dwellings huddled together between the boundaries of these two satanic mills, enjoying no vista beyond the grimy spike-topped tannery yard wall.

On that spring night so long ago, John Kemp, tenant of the central two up, two down cottage, lay restless in his bed, all sleep denied him for all that he had completed a long hard journey the previous evening, helping an old drover take a large flock of sheep across country to their summer grazing in the distant rain-washed hills.

Droving was not John's chosen calling. From the days of early childhood he had been instructed in the craft of wood carving by his travelling father, a proud man who could boast that the carved swingboats shown in the Crystal Palace as part of Queen Victoria's 1851 Great Exhibition had started out as blocks of timber in his hands.

Childhood for John had been one long carefree adventure, summer travelling in the beautiful ornate waggon that had been the envy of every Romany eye that beheld it. Each autumn John's father returned to their winter quarters, a snug stone quarry under the woods, working there with home-made lathes and unsophisticated tools beneath a lean-to shelter, where craftsmanship brought carefully seasoned wood to life.

John grew to manhood developing the same skill and artistry as his father, knowing that he must leave the wandering life if he intended to marry his pretty Emily. Her house-dwelling parents did all they could to discourage her from marrying someone they regarded as a 'half-wild gippo', but their offhand attitude paled into insignificance by comparison with the reactions from John's family.

The night before the wedding day, cousins, uncles, brothers and other, far-flung members of his family foregathered to dissuade him from going ahead with his marriage, pleading with him not to marry a 'gorgio rachli', adjourning to the Gate Inn to get him drunk enough to see reason. When this failed they knocked him down to shake his brains to rights in their futile efforts to make him change his mind.

John could recall every detail of that scene, illuminated only by the flames of the campfire. For the last time his father asked him to renounce the girl. John stayed firm. Sadly the older man called for bowl and water. Washing his hands with ritualistic thoroughness, he announced that as from that moment, John's taint was erased from the family memory. His son was worse than dead. The bowl was smashed, the towel and soap burned on the bonfire, for they too were now 'morchardi', evil and unclean.

With his sack of carpentry tools on his back, John walked away from his much-loved family. They watched him going with solemn faces, as if they were turned to stone.

Two against the world, John brought his bride to the two up, two down hovel of No. 3 Swain's Passage, combatting cockroaches, rats, lice and bedbugs with the unorthodox remedies and treatments of his race in the only place they could find at the rent they could afford.

During the years that followed, those having contact with Smiling Johnny respected him for his honesty, cheerful countenance and willingness to work until he dropped to earn a shilling or two to feed his ever-increasing family.

Only Emily knew how the claustrophobic atmosphere of Swain's Passage so overwhelmed him at times that he would slip away after dark and walk for miles under the night sky with the grass wet under his bare feet.

John Kemp soon earned a reputation as a craftsman wood carver and joiner amongst house builders now erecting fashionably large houses and villas in the city, but this did not mean that he could rely on regular work. There were times when he was glad to make crates for the soap works at a penny a box.

Another opportunity for extra earnings came from twice-weekly city cattle-market days. John could expect to earn a few shillings portering, penning cattle, and marking them with their sale numbers. Livestock were then brought to market on the hoof. Cows that were to be sold were left unmilked on market day morning to enlarge the size of their udders, a practice causing the animal some discomfort and stress. This needed to be relieved before the buyer took them home. Johnny was usually at hand, complete with milking pails, and the oldest boy and girl of his family to take the precious liquid home.

Occasionally John was asked to help the professional drovers to take auctioned sheep, cattle, pigs or even geese flocks to some near or distant destination. On that springtime night when yellow fog sprawled a foul-smelling blanket across the river area of the city, John lay restless in the stiflingly small front bedroom in Swain's Passage, telling his heavily pregnant wife about the beautiful spring blossoming countryside he had walked through during his latest droving mission, Emily being too uncomfortable to find peaceful sleep.

Somewhere along the tannery wall, a blackbird began his prelude to the dawn chorus.

'Listen to that daft-brained bird,' John muttered. 'It has all the world to sing in, yet it chooses to sing here in this stinking midden. We have no choice, nor have we any wings to fly away.'

Through the thin partition wall came the sounds of a violent bedroom argument between their next-door neighbours, and the almost incessant coughing of a consumptive child.

'Poor little soul,' Emily sighed. 'When Midwife Aunt Hannah came to see me today, she told me young Iris has no chance of seeing the fall of leaf in the autumn. She is wasting away so fast. We are lucky, Johnny. Even if we are often on the verge of pawning my wedding ring to fill our brood's bellies, our children stay healthy, while so many children around here die off with disease.'

'If I could make money as easily as I make strong babies, I would take you away from this benighted place,' John told her. 'At this moment, out beyond the city, there's a full round, pumpkin moon shining down over the hills and countryside. Last night I could see this town fog like a dirty rag of flannel down here in the valley basin, while I sat with old Drover Merrill under a wild cherry tree in full blossom in the moonlight. Tomorrow will be the time of Maying, yet there are over thirty young ones here in Swain's Passage who never see a bluebell or a hawthorn tree in bloom. Emily, I can't lay abed and let that happen on this May Day morning. Can you get the children up early? Put on the girls' white pinafores and have them looking tidy. Tell all the other kids that Jack-in-the-Green is going to take them Maying, and ask Iris's mother to get her dressed. She is going to be our May Queen.'

'Johnny Kemp, we've been married twenty years and have had twelve children, yet you can still surprise me. You are still a travelling man at heart.'

Within minutes of leaving his bed, John was hurrying along beside the open sewer river in the long-drawn-out birthing of a foggy dawn. He left the city boundaries behind him, climbing a moonlit woodland path, working speedily to fashion several small hazelwood posy baskets, cutting slender branches to form a large dome-shaped woven frame. The rising sun was thinning the mist before John completed the task he set out to do.

He returned to the riverside alleys of the city with his hawthorn-blossom-bedecked frame around him, the flower-filled posy baskets swinging from a long pole balanced over one shoulder, singing as he walked. A street trader gladly lent John Kemp a barrow when he knew the purpose it was to serve.

An old woman who sold ribbons and laces from her stall in the

Long Market, found streams of flags and bunting in her backyard shed to decorate the handcart. John made a few more calls, wheedling for the charitable gifts of backstreet traders before returning to Swain's Passage.

Children from along the terrace ran out to greet him as if he had the Pied Piper's power to charm them from their houses.

Consumptive Iris, who had lain for weeks in the bedroom she shared with her parents and three sisters, now rested enthroned in a cushioned chair, all wrapped round in Emily's best white hand-made lace bedspread, as John placed a crown of wild May blossoms on her head. If his hands were torn with a few splinters of the hawthorn, it was of no consequence. One little girl, who had lain waiting to die, was for that one spring morning a May Queen on whom the sun now shone.

All flower bedecked and hauling the May Queen's chariot with their ribboned streamers, the laughing children set off to parade around the city streets, John leading the May Day procession, dancing along beneath his Jack-in-the-Green framework of branches playing his penny whistle, his antics making the children laugh.

He took them through the Dane John park where he produced a special May Day treat donated by a kindly baker who had given him a sackful of stale cakes. When they came back through the narrow streets to the Butter Market Cross they caused some slight confusion in the busy horse-drawn traffic. An irate gentleman in a carriage called a pair of patrolling constables to disperse the little rabble. The children sang and danced.

When John explained that this was likely to be their May Queen's last summer, the constables relayed the message to the cross-looking gentleman.

As a crowd gathered, a tweed-suited man called out, 'Come on, you miserable blighters. This chap is trying to help these poor little devils. I'm passing around my hat.'

The man in the carriage beckoned John towards him.

'Is that child receiving proper medical treatment? Bring her to this address at ten tomorrow morning. Now move your brats aside. I need to get to Longport Street straight away.'

John had never learned his letters. The policeman told him that the gentleman was the chief surgeon of the city hospital.

John encountered much ignorant fear and suspicion that Iris

was being lured into a place where doctors experimented on poor people, cutting them open just to practise using their knives, but her mother agreed that Iris would die soon if she was not given this opportunity. Thus did Johnny's chance encounter with a gentleman in a hurry give one small girl the prospect of a long life.

The coins that passers-by had thrown to the raggle-taggle children came to a fair amount of money. Knowing that his feckless neighbours would spend their children's share on beer, bets or gin, Smiling John led his followers to a second-hand clothes shop, owned by a good-hearted woman known as Aunt Hannah, who also served the community as the untrained but well-practised midwife to the poor.

Every child went home with new second-hand boots. Honest John Kemp handed the remaining ninepence to Iris's mother to give the child extra food.

Smiling John Kemp was not to know that one small hawthorn splinter in a finger could cause a healthy man to endure an agonized, blood-poisoned death just one week later.

Thus did John Kemp, my maternal grandfather, spend the forty-second and last May Day of his life, a long long time ago.

Femme Fatale with Spots

Many a keen young man casually ringing to engage one of my older sisters in trivial small talk on the telephone found his romantic aspirations suddenly cut short by Dad's hand depressing the receiver arm. He regarded such usage of the awesome instrument on the passage wall by the kitchen door as utterly frivolous. The telephone was for important matters, such as the price of porkers in the fat stock market, or for summoning the vet.

To my mother, any unexpected telephone call was like an unopened telegram, conjuring fears of family disasters and sudden death.

Early one summer morning, the telephone rang as I was humping two full milking pails along the passage towards the dairy. Shooing away a couple of cajoling cats that purred around my ankles, I set down the pails and lifted the receiver, calling to

Mum that Aunt Bertha was on the line. Convinced that some dire tragedy had overtaken her sister-in-law, my cottage-loaf-shaped Mum came bustling from the kitchen, mentally preparing for the worst.

Aunt Bertha's reassurance that Uncle Fred and Cousin Daisy were well, and that the drapery store they owned had not been burned down, burgled, or declared bankrupt, made Mum question Aunt Bertha's reasons for bothering to ring at all.

With the cats becoming increasingly interested in the milk pails, I left Mum to it. She was smiling when I went back to the kitchen, so I knew that none of our innumerable relatives had died.

'Guess what, Jo,' she said happily. 'Your Uncle Fred and Aunt Bertha are shutting the shop and treating the staff to their yearly outing tomorrow. Your aunt has rung to ask if you would like to keep Daisy company. Isn't that good of her?'

Little involving Cousin Daisy or her condescending mother and father could make me joyful, and I said so. As a prospering city draper, smug Uncle Fred grew more pompous as his girth and bank balance increased. He regarded my father as a tiller of the soil, while Aunt Bertha lost no opportunity to compare Mum's hard-working country life with her own.

Domineering and shrewish, she ruled her husband with a rod of iron, acting imperiously towards all those in her employ. The couple's one susceptibility was towards their daughter. From childhood Daisy demanded the creamiest cakes on the plate, the most expensive toys, and the prettiest dresses. Eighteen months my senior and with her eighteenth birthday approaching, Daisy was unmanageable, overweight and man mad. I told Mum I would prefer a day spent cleaning out the fowl houses to a seaside jaunt with our city relatives, but she persisted.

'Look, Jo, it is no quick trip to the beach and a plate of cockles. They are spending most of the day cruising on a paddle steamer. Your aunt has paid for your ticket and for the special evening meal at a hotel, so it would be extremely bad-mannered not to go. It sometimes worries me that you have so few days away from the farm, so I'm asking you to accept, just to please me.'

Put like that I seemed to have no option other than to comply. Having phoned my acceptance, Mum enlightened me to the fact that the early start to the day would necessitate my staying with Aunt Bertha that night, and the next after the trip ended. Any enthusiasm I had tried to muster vanished as fast as summer snow, but Mum seemed anxious that I should not miss out on this unusual beanfeast, so I hitched a lift into the city with the oil, soap, and candle chandler, whose van happened to be passing on his fortnightly round.

He set me down in the main city square at about six that evening. Clutching a carrier bag and probably reeking of carbolic soap and paraffin, I walked into Aunt Bertha and Uncle Fred's drapery emporium just as a pale spotty-faced girl in a hideously shapeless black dress was altering the sign on the door.

'We're closing' she sniffed. I explained that I had come to see her employers.

'If you're hoping for the post of Junior on the dress materials counter, the old trout is a slave driver, and watch out for the boss if you're using the steps to get the rolls of silk from off the top shelf. He's liable to dart up behind you, trying to give two helping hands.'

Bearing down on us in a black rustling dress with a mass of white organdie round the neck like a pie frill round a ham bone, Aunt Bertha berated me for not ringing the side door bell, and reminded the young assistant that several altered garments were waiting to be pressed and delivered before any of the staff would be allowed to go home, bearing in mind that the drapery emporium would be closed all the next day.

Completely out of my element, I followed Aunt Bertha up the stairs to her living quarters and felt uncomfortably embarrassed to be served a pinch-penny meal by a skinny kid who looked no more than twelve years old, but must have been a fourteen-year-old school leaver.

'Yes, ma'am. No, ma'am' – bobbing up and down in a ridiculously ugly cap and apron, the poor girl looked as if life had defeated her before it had really begun. Self-important Uncle Fred ignored the girl completely as Aunt Bertha queened it at the head of the table. Cousin Daisy just sat and ate.

Appalled that I had no more suitable outfit for the proposed sea trip than the clothes I was wearing, Aunt Bertha sorted through Daisy's vast wardrobe, but Daisy was short and fat, while I was tall and skinny.

Uncle Fred remembered a purple and gold tube-like frock that had remained unsold throughout their last sale. It fitted where it touched me, so I was taken down to the fitting room where a middle-aged woman was stitching black veiling around a black hat.

'When you have that funeral order finished, take a couple of darts in this, and put a false hem on it,' Aunt Bertha ordered.

Alone with the milliner, I learned that she had a war-blinded husband waiting for her to go home. Trying tactfully to reject the finished garment, I told Aunt Bertha I could not accept her dress on top of all the other hospitality she was offering.

'You stupid clodhopper,' Daisy sneered. 'You've only been asked because there are two spare places now that Miss Mussell from underwear has gone down with chickenpox and that new girl has walked out. 'Ma thinks it will stop me having a good time with you as my watchdog. That's why you're here. Aunt Flo has the other ticket. The miserable old crow is going to keep an eye on the food baskets and generally put a blight on us all.'

It was the first time I had spent a night in the city and I was amazed at the number of people abroad long after country people reckoned to go to bed. There were drunks and females shouting in darkened doorways. A street sign shone intermittently across my face as I tried to sleep on a camp bed in Daisy's room. She enlarged on the more lurid details of a love affair conducted secretly in the shop basement, where the young man in charge of Soft Furnishings and Household Linens held sway. I longed for the safe country darkness of my own home.

Council men clattering around the streets with water carts to wash down pavements and roadways heralded the noisy dawn. Milkmen sang, newsboys whistled, maids scrubbed doorsteps, and I was up dressed and ready for the outing long before the rest of the household were awake.

An open-topped charabanc arrived bedecked with red, white and blue streamers and painted banners to tell the world we were the drapery store staff outing. Uncle Fred, in boater and striped blazer, escorted his resplendently dressed wife to the seat beside the driver. Aunt Flo, clad in her usual funeral frock, sat directly behind them, turning around and casting frequent disapproving glances as the shop girls called out to anything male between nine and ninety, provided it moved.

Daisy managed to share our seat with her latest Romeo, the weedy youth from Household Linens, with dandruff and a celluloid collar topping a grubby shirt. I moved back to a vacant seat, cheering up as we rode out across country, heading for the jetty of a small, select coastal resort.

Never having been on board any seagoing vessel larger than a rowing boat, to me the brightly painted paddle steamer seemed enormous as it came alongside the quay. There were dozens of others waiting to embark, but Uncle Fred fussed around as if his female employees were members of his harem.

Judging by some of the comments I had overheard about the assistant in Ladies' Underwear, whose chickenpox had given me the opportunity to take part in this outing, this was not far short of the mark.

Aunt Flo bullied a member of the ship's crew into stacking our food hampers under the companionway amidships and sat guarding them with a gimlet eye. Every day of my life I had looked out to the wide waters of the estuary from our upland fields, so I left Daisy to her own devices and went on to the upper deck to try to pinpoint my own home, but the hills were shrouded in lowering cloud. A stiff breeze whipped up white horses on the wave crests and for the next couple of hours I strolled around the ship, imagining I was enjoying a luxury cruise.

That which had been only a smudge of land on the horizon on clear days, or a cluster of twinkling lights in the dark, turned out to be a bright and bustling, funfair-infested resort as we drew alongside the end of a long pier. Somehow I was left to help Aunt Flo carry an extremely heavy hamper, and by reason of the fact that she refused to carry it any farther, our party ate their picnic lunch close by the pier on the sands.

Some of the girls donned daring sleeveless bathing suits and rubber hats to splash, scream and paddle at the tide's edge. Aunt Flo declared she had never before seen such depravity, or so sin-ridden a place in all her life.

The velocity of the wind increased as we waited to board the ship for the return journey. The vessel pitched and rolled, sending most passengers down below. Aunt Flo, convinced that Divine Judgement had condemned the rest of us to death by drowning, sat by the deck railings near a lifebelt, determined to be saved. In the saloon, Uncle Fred complained of feeling itchy and poorly, wondering how to explain away a rash identical to his absent Ladies' Underwear assistant's chickenpox.

An irate ship's officer came complaining about Daisy's outrageous conduct towards a member of his crew and somehow I was blamed for not staying with her all the time.

There was little singing in the charabanc after we landed, but as we headed for the country hotel where we were to have dinner, I remembered something that cheered me up. Risking worrying Mum by telephone so late at night, I borrowed twopence and rang to tell her that the last bus to the village would pass by within ten minutes. I could be home by ten o'clock. My city relatives were too busy arguing to worry over my departure. I left them to their watery soup and waited by the bus stop in the friendly darkness.

We saw no more of our affluent relatives until one August afternoon, but with half the harvest still waiting to be gathered, there was no time for social niceties or entertaining visitors. Watching Uncle Fred's Austin Ruby car puttering along the farm lane, Dad expressed his displeasure in a few forthright, unprintable words. My mother had just brought out a jug of hot tea and as she stood beside the wheat rick we were stacking in the yard, she offered the peaceable suggestion that her brother had closed his drapery store early, and driven over from town to lend us a helping hand.

Dad's pithy reply is best politely summarized as being 'highly unlikely'.

Seeing that Uncle Fed had brought Aunt Bertha and Cousin Daisy with him, we held a brief whispered conversation about the reasons for this unexpected visit. The trio looked excessively gloomy. In fact, Daisy was blotchy-faced and weeping as she lounged along the back seat. Lacking finesse, Dad called to Uncle Fred as he alighted from the car, asking point-blank why they had come.

Because my corpulent uncle aspired towards the higher reaches of town society, my parents attributed his pale lard-like, pudgy features to the civic feasts and functions that his position as a town councillor forced him to attend. As he stumped across our yard, his face was more purple than pallid, and it was obvious that he was in a flaming rage.

'Stay where you are, girl!' he hollered to his weeping daughter.

In ordinary circumstances that remark alone would have merited a sound ticking off from Aunt Bertha, but as she flustered out of the car, she dabbed her eyes through the spotted veil adorning the artificial flower garden of a hat perched on the upper ridges of her iron-waved hair.

Flinging her arms forth in a grand dramatic gesture, she approached my startled mother.

'Liza,' she cried, 'will you show compassion on our time of torment? Save Daisy and our good name!'

At this time my parents thought that my absence might be politic, but Uncle Fred said gruffly, 'If we are to keep control of this situation, your Jo will have to help.'

Hardly daring to contemplate the cause of the family crisis, Mum asked what all the commotion was about.

Quivering with righteous indignation, Aunt Bertha announced tragically, 'We have just found out that Daisy has been pursued.'

My parents exchanged the kind of glances that told each other volumes, my outspoken father bluntly asking the inevitable question.

'Daisy pursued? The crux of the matter is in knowing if she's been caught.'

My aunt was prone to highly dramatic head- and heart-clutching attacks, known to Dad as 'Old Bertha's gasping staggers'. His comments made another spasm seem highly likely until Uncle Fred handed her a bottle of smelling salts from her handbag.

'Pay no heed to such crudity, dearest. Farm-bred people tend to be extremely coarse.'

Ignoring Dad, Aunt Bertha took my mother around the far side of the stack and beckoned me to follow. As she drew a folded letter from her handbag, she admitted that Daisy did not know she had found this missive in her wardrobe. Blushing scarlet, she held it forth for Mum to read. My own experience of romantic notes was confined to the letters that the blacksmith's son wrote from the various RAF bases where he was stationed, but these were more concerned with colour blindness tests, issue boots and interminable courses than with passionate declarations of adoration and love.

By comparison, the letter from Daisy's new sweetheart was a

sizzling epic, but the thought of my plump cousin inspiring anyone to lie sleepless, filled with overwhelming torment until the writer could cover her with kisses, only invoked in me the unkind but uncontrollable desire to laugh.

My mother was not laughing. In her gentle-hearted wisdom she knew that if Daisy was really in trouble, her parents were so afflicted with 'suburbanitis' they would reject her out of hand for fear of what their associates might say. Walking back to Dad, Mum looked at Daisy who sat trying to console herself with nutty nougat bars and a pile of *Poppy's Weekly* magazines, then said she could stay with us for a while to sort herself out.

By this time Dad was stamping around like a fidgety horse in a swarm of hornets. Harvesting stopped for no one, and if we were to stay solvent we must resume our work.

'I'll make a business deal with you Harry,' Uncle Fred said briskly. 'If you can get this damned dago-looking Romeo out of Daisy's way so that she starts acting reasonably, I'll finance you for as much cash as you need to tide you over until your corn is safely threshed and sold.'

Both Dad and I were pretty subdued as we worked out in the wheat field loading the waggon, shocked that anyone could transform parental anxiety into a business transaction.

I stood among the sheaves I was loading, looking at my dependable rock-like father, the fields, the valleys, and out towards the blue waters of the estuary that had beckoned all through the hard, nonstop working days of a hot summer, and knew again that I would want no other parents, nor to change my way of living, for all the wealth and social power in the world.

After the boat fiasco, I made it clear that I would be no one's watchdog. Daisy was older than me and it was time she could sort out the male species into sheep or goats.

For all that there were several spare rooms where she could have sat up in bed reading the *Picturegoer* magazines by candle-light, Daisy was sure that the house was haunted and demanded to share my room. I doubt if anyone who worked from sunrise until dark pitching or stacking corn sheaves ever suffered from insomnia. By the time my harvesting day was finished, every fibre of my being ached for sleep. Daisy sat up in her bed, dying to relate the saga of her thwarted passion, her salmon-pink vest showing beneath a frilly nightie of apricot-coloured crepe de Chine.

I tried to keep awake for it had never been my lot to hear a first-hand account of being so soundly kissed by Ramon Navarro's double in the back row of the pictures that the St John Ambulance nurse on duty had to render first aid. Sheer fatigue made me start snuffling like a hibernating hedgehog until Daisy woke me to say that it was no wonder that while she wore silk undies and seldom soiled her hands, I was as sunburned as a gipsy, worked like a navvy, wore cotton nighties in bed and, what was more unladylike, I snored.

Perhaps I should have shown a more tolerant attitude, but it seemed to me that if she was being chased by some six-foot-tall lover, all Latin masculinity and muscles, Uncle Fred and Aunt Bertha should count their blessings and marry her off quickly. Looking at dumpy Daisy shovelling face cream on her sallow, oily skin, I was sure so golden an opportunity would not come knocking twice.

Mum took Daisy under her gentle wing, keeping her occupied with the various old folk-lore beauty hints she could remember.

It was nothing to find Daisy recumbent under the copper beech tree with cucumber and egg white plastered over her face.

At last the harvest fields were empty, but before apple picking started and the field crop of potatoes was lifted, there was one more place I intended to go. I was determined to cycle down to the seashore that had taunted me for weeks. Daisy wanted to come with me. She rode my old 'sit up and beg' model. I borrowed the blacksmith's bike.

It was hardly Brighton, just a bus stop, a few beach huts and a café, but it had all that I looked for. Daisy suddenly announced that she had phoned her Latin-type lover from the village phone box and that he would come and find us on the beach. I knew there was nothing I could do should Daisy's magnificent male drag her off among the dunes, so I wriggled into my stockinet bathing suit and walked with Daisy down the beach for a doggy-paddle swim. I drew her attention to a weedy-looking individual standing watching from the sea wall.

She ran towards him, squawking, 'Coo-ee! Ernie!'

He simpered at us, all bad teeth and acne, uttering the romantic greeting: ''Ullo, Dais. Fancy a pint of winkles?' If this was her idea of pulsating passion, she needed glasses. There was no way he could be mistaken for a film lover.

We planned to picnic after another swim, but he had no bathing trunks. Daisy persuaded him to paddle, so he stood on the sand, rolling up the trouser legs of his grubby blue suit, explaining that the crepe bandage around his calf was a precautionary measure against the shop assistant's curse and torment, varicose veins.

Removing his boots and smelly unwashed socks, he displayed pink corn plasters on each grimy, long-nailed toe. It was all too much for my weird sense of humour, so I rushed down to the tideway where only the gulls could see my mirth.

Daisy was very quiet as we rode back to the farm. The next morning she expressed the opinion that a neighbouring farmer, known to have the morals of a randy cockerel, showed all the film-star charm of the actor Leslie Howard. She asked if I could think up any excuse for her to meet him. Mum quickly decided that Daisy could now be safely returned home.

The Weather House

U ntil the local authority policy makers decided that the
educational needs of all Tylers End children were best
served by sending them to a vast newly erected urban
school some six or seven miles distant, the teaching of the hamlet's youngsters had been the main purpose of Miss Harriet
Meadow's long working life.

For over three decades, shy, apprehensive infants starting
school for the first time were introduced to the 'magic' of Miss
Meadow's antique toy weather house, and in small integrated
groups that might well include brothers, sisters, or a couple of
cousins, they stopped crying for their mothers and lost their fear
of school.

Miss Meadow's school roll seldom aspired far beyond thirty,
even in the height of the fruit-picking season when children

from itinerant travelling families boosted the numbers and brought the recurring problem of nits.

This gave her an insight into each pupil's standard of health and academic capabilities. She understood the village women's problems of finding the money for adequate footwear, warm clothing, and enough food to bring up their families on ludicrously low agricultural wages.

Knowing many family secrets of the Tylers End inhabitants, Miss Meadow was blessed with the wisdom to keep her knowledge to herself, doing good by stealth, always ready to do battle with anyone, from strap-wielding sadistic fathers to the chairman of the County Council, if the welfare of any of her pupils was involved.

With the closure of the village school, the children of Tylers End congregated at the lane end without shelter, awaiting a bus that was supposed to collect them at a quarter to eight each morning. It was frequently half an hour late in arriving to take them to the various infant, junior, or senior departments of a vast urban school, tiny tadpoles in a stream of over fourteen hundred pupils from the town. They now had teachers by the score, elusive beings who seldom knew enough about individual boys and girls to identify them by name.

When the old village school and Miss Meadow were both deemed redundant, she was allowed to purchase the tiny schoolhouse, the adjoining schoolroom, the school garden and playground to enlarge her home. As a retirement gift, a group of her ex-pupils transformed the old playground and school vegetable plot into a landscaped flower garden, encouraging a hobby that now filled the empty hours of what had once been such a busy life.

The antique toy weather house still occupied the place of honour on the same sunny south-facing schoolroom windowsill, now transformed into Miss Meadow's lounge. Sometimes when she sat resting in her armchair, she recalled various incidents, remembering the day of ink monitor Lily Palming's upshooting hand and urgent request to be excused from lessons for five minutes at the most.

'Please, Miss, it's going to rain and my Mum has gone over to Cuckoopint Bottoms to nurse Mr Bendle's poorly leg and clear the place up for him. Before she went, she pegged three copper loads of washing out to dry on the clotheslines. It would take a month of Sundays to mangle, starch, and dry it all again. Can I run home and take it in, Miss? Your little man has just popped out of the weather house with his umbrella. Please, Miss, can I go, Miss? I won't be longer than a couple of shakes of a gnat's backside!'

Lily, now a plump grandmother who still came to help with the housework for an hour every morning, was then the eldest daughter of a hard-working widow. She kept her promise on that long-gone day, thankful to have safely reached the shelter of the schoolroom before a sudden summer storm spat lightning, thunder and a torrential cloud burst from the sky. Of such events were the legends about the schoolroom weather house woven, some pupils and their parents taking the mysterious movements of the little carved figures more seriously than most.

As Miss Meadow sat in sun-blessed warmth looking out by the window, Ben Loamer walked back into her memory. Gangling, spindle-shanked Ben, always two sizes larger than his clothes, head and shoulders taller than his teacher, with size thirteen boots and the two-coloured mop of sun-bleached hair that stood on end no matter how his mother tried to tame it into tidiness with water, spit, or melted lard.

Ben's tenant farmer father was often teetering on the tightrope of financial disaster, his need for a decent hay crop and successful harvest very crucial indeed. As Ben lumbered into school one bright summer morning, Miss Meadow noticed that he was transferring a businesslike looking hammer from his lunch bag to his desk.

Her questioning brought forth the reluctant admission: 'Please, Miss, our top hayfield has been mowed ten days and we have been raking and turning 'un all weekend. It will be fit to load and stack come dew rise this morning, so Father told me to keep a sharp eye on your weather house. If the little old man pokes his 'yud outside to make it rain, I've got to take this 'ere yammer and knock the sod back in again.'

Miss Meadow remembered being far less accommodating towards Ben's ideas than she had been to Lily Palming. Every year that passed convinced her that the little wooden lady in the weather house had much in common with herself.

Fading with age, creaking of joint, and increasingly aware of her own antiquity, she too stayed indoors whenever the tiny wet weather man emerged from his little wooden house with his umbrella, to stare lugubriously at the sky. When clear skies brought the brightly painted little lady out to linger amongst her perpetually blooming little wooden flowers, Miss Meadow went out into the garden to enjoy the sunshine too.

Surrounded by the scent of honeysuckle and the sound of bird song, she sat by the open window marvelling at the yearly miracle of summer in a country garden, wondering where all the youth-eroding years had flown. Was it really so long ago that she embarked on that first anxious journey to Tylers End, alighting for the first time from the little puffing billy steam train that once chugged along the branch line between sea and city, stopping 'at request' at Tylers Halt?

She remembered still the ticket collector-cum-porter, station master and level crossing keeper's look of incredulity as she asked if her trunks might be delivered to the schoolhouse, and his frosty reply that if she was the new schoolmaster's daughter, her father had not yet arrived, although the vicar of the three surrounding parishes had taken the trouble to drive over to meet him at the Halt.

Scraping her hair up under her hat in an attempt to look more mature, and trying to keep control of the situation, she stalked between the milk churns and crates of fruit and vegetables with as much dignity as she could muster.

Miss Meadow hoped she sounded more self-assured than she felt as she answered, 'I think the reverend gentleman is waiting for me!'

'Don't make any hasty decisions, miss,' the railwayman had warned anxiously. 'Best let me store your trunks at my place, just there by the level crossing, until you decide if you're stopping. Three other gentleman teachers came with their wives but decided to give Tylers End school a wide berth. The school has been closed since Easter! You must be their last hope.'

Doubts now joined forces with Miss Meadow's earlier astonishment that her application for the post of Head Teacher had been granted without the formality of an interview. That first glance at the vicar's patched jacket and gaunt appearance confirmed her growing conviction that her new pupils would not be the offspring of the idle rich. Brushing aside her eagerness to see the school and adjoining schoolhouse, the vicar insisted that she must first meet the school patrons, governors and parochial worthies foregathered at The Vicarage to take afternoon tea.

Fortified only by stale sandwiches and dry seed cake, she fended off a minor inquisition. Any romantic entanglements? Her emphatic negative answer denied busybody probing people any knowledge that her hopes of a happy future had been incinerated in a crashed aircraft funeral pyre, or that if dreams had become reality, she would have been the bride of a Royal Flying Corps pilot a few months before.

When the grief-crazed belief that Frank would somehow rise phoenix-like from the ashes gave way to a sense of inadequacy and despair, she had known that hard work alone would numb the cold, empty misery threatening to overwhelm her.

It had been this sense of desperation that had made her apply for the less then remotely possible chance of gaining a head teacher's post in the depths of the country, light years away from the world she had once known.

No! Definitely no! There were no emotional commitments. All she had left to carry her through life was a bundle of letters, a silver wings brooch, an old flying jacket, and the quaint antique weather house Frank had bought for her from a street market stall on his last leave.

He had joked then that it would probably be the only house they would be able to call their own for years. Now she was being questioned about her willingness to live in a schoolhouse on her own.

The suggestion that she might see the school was countered by the information that temporary lodgings had been arranged for her. Suspecting some sort of conspiracy, she asked if she might take a quick exploratory stroll around the churchyard. There she had spoken to a woman putting flowers on a grave.

'School House is just down the lane, round the corner. Nobody lives there. Who would risk it when two teachers and seven children have been buried in this graveyard during the last four years?'

Realizing why she had been appointed, Miss Meadow considered a quick retreat, but the tiny schoolhouse was one of the prettiest cottages she had ever seen. Furious from her quick tour of inspection, she had returned to confront the local bigwigs at

The Vicarage, demanding that they accompany her and decide how the place could be made safe.

Sitting in her armchair, the old lady smiled at the recollection of her young self leading the school governors through waist-high stinging nettles to insist that the cesspits of the yard latrines be filled with quicklime, and that her first action as school mistress was to smash the cast-iron hand pump that had oozed green slimy water into the cloakroom stone sink.

How she had toiled in those few weeks before the school re-opened. She had carried water from a safe well for the first two years at Tylers End, and probably used more soap and disinfectant than blackboard chalk. Realizing that this determined young woman cared for their children's welfare, the village folk began to lend a helping hand.

Dwelling on the wartime years, the old teacher remembered the evacuee children that for a while doubled her numbers. Some still wrote to her. So many children, sons and daughters of her early pupils, all helping to fill the void left by her own un-born dreams.

Sometimes of late, on mornings such as this, she experienced a strange roaring noise in her head that played tricks with her sight and even made the weather house on the window sill difficult to keep in focus. The noise suddenly increased to the scream of a plunging aircraft engine, becoming unbearable until there was suddenly a breathless silence, and a clear radiant light.

The weather house now seemed much larger, with the smiling sunshine lady still there amongst her wooden flowers. Of the wet weather man there was no sign. In his place was the much-loved, vividly remembered figure in Royal Flying Corps uniform, standing with arms outstretched.

When Lily Palming came to house clean a few hours later, she found Miss Meadow on the floor, clutching the weather house.

'So fond of that old thing, she was,' sobbed Lily to the local policeman. 'It's a funny thing, though. You remember the little old man who came out when it was going to rain? The weather house doesn't seem to have broken, but I can't see him any-where.'

Going Courting

Before farm mechanization changed the pattern of life and 'the pill' meant usually a wonder cure for constipation and other forms of stomach disorder, large families abounded in rural communities who still looked for their living to the labour-intensive land.

The birth of a boy was regarded as cause for rejoicing. Sons could lend a helping hand from an early age and eventually supplement the parental earnings as farm-labouring lads, or by working on the family holding. Either way they could reasonably be expected to offer the reassurance of support and comfort in their parents' old age.

Daughters were a totally different matter. The creed of female inferiority propounded down through generations was passed on in the village classroom and in Sunday school. Many a cottager's daughter was brought up to 'know her place' and accept that a good situation in domestic service was the limit of personal ambition beyond which she could not hope to aspire, no matter how bright and intelligent she was.

Humility was the attribute she should strive for until such time as she could find someone willing to call her wife, after which she must honour her promise to obey. The most dreadful prospect a girl could face was the stigma of being 'left on the shelf', to waste away into a grim penurious future of rejection as a withered old maid.

On small farms relying on the tenant's family to supply the entire workforce, parental connivance was frequently the main contributory factor in bringing a young couple together, or conversely ensuring that 'unsuitable' matches were kept apart, long-standing family feuds in insular inbred rural communities being rife.

Gaining Father's permission to walk out with a young man as the prelude to being allowed to 'go courting' frequently presented formidable hurdles for a girl to overcome. Any starry-eyed romantic notions she might hold of being placed on a pedestal and cherished by an as yet unknown Romeo had as much chance of survival as a tender orchid seedling in a sharp frost.

All too frequently the rites of romance had all the affection, gallantry, and finesse of market horse traders bargaining over an unbroken filly, discussing her potential abilities for hard work and breeding, seeking assurances that she was good-tempered, sound in teeth, wind, and limb, and would not need handling with a firm rein.

Parental restrictions, enforced with a dogged determination to keep flighty daughters from straying could have the reverse effect; furtive defiance frequently resulted in a nine-days' scandal and a shotgun wedding. There were some girls who either evaded or escaped the attentions of the local likely lads, making the most of their unattached freedom while managing to allay parental fears that they might never be led to the altar steps. Libby, daughter of Thirza and Horace Hookersley was a case in point.

Horace believed in keeping a strict watch on Libby, who had worked as a daily maid to an elderly widow from the time she left the village school. Libby was only allowed to attend occasional weekday church- and chapel-organized entertainments, the firm understanding being that she must be home by 9. 30 at the latest,

Horace being convinced that most evils of this world lurked ready to pounce on those choosing to stay out of their homes and their beds after ten o'clock at night.

On the night Libby went to a missionary magic lantern meeting in the village hall, her mother sat in her straight-backed wooden chair all evening, anxiously waiting for her daughter as the hours wore on. Thirza listened intently for the sound of Libby's footsteps across the paved yard, but the only noises to disturb the silence came from her husband snoring by the fireside, and the inexorable ticking of the old mantel clock.

The clock chiming ten roused Horace to awareness and irritability. Methodically unlacing his heavy farm boots and placing them to dry on the fender, he glanced around the kitchen.

'Where be our Libby then? 'Tis well past ten! Light the candle, and put out the lamp, Mother. I'll not be flouted further. It is long past time for wholesome folk to be safely asleep in bed. Put you the guard up to the fire, while I bolt the door.'

Thirza remonstrated that they could not go to bed when some harm might have befallen Libby.

'Get them boots back on, man, and see if there is any sign of her torchlight bobbing along the lane. She's mortal frit of the dark if truth be told. She only went to the magic lantern show because it was supposed to be of an improving nature. She could be laying half murdered and hollering in a ditch.'

Horace answered that if Libby put her mind to hollering, she would easily be heard on the far side of the parish. If she was lying in a ditch at this moment, he would wager that she was not alone. He dismissed Thirza's reproach for such stockyard coarseness.

'That girl have been acting middling strange, Mother. You told me yourself that she spent three months' savings to buy elastic stays that scrunch female insides all together. Our Libby looked like a bulging bag of bran tied round the middle, when she set out tonight. I caught her using the cattle market prices page of the local paper to test that her curling tongs would not frizzle her hair off. I blame all them moving picture shows and wireless sets for making young people get so wayward and out of hand.'

Thirza argued that if some lad was courting Libby, she had

shown no signs of it. The girl had not gone dreamy, daft, moon-struck, or off her food. Come to think of it, she had never shown much interest in men.

'More's the pity,' Horace retorted acidly. 'I used to look forward to the time when all them young cockerels would come crowing around our spring chicken, eager to help with the farm work to earn my approval and show off their muscles, but Libby be that plain she hasn't even attracted any widowed old roosters yet!'

Thirza said that this proved her point. Libby was not likely to be encouraging strange men to lead her astray. Horace would do better to take himself along Foxley Bottoms to find out why she had not come home.

'Missus!' Horace bellowed in the same tone of voice that brought his hogs to the feeding trough. 'I'm mortal tired! I'm bolting the door this moment. It will do the young madam no harm to spend the night in the cowshed if she can't come home at a respectable time.'

Hearing the click of the back door latch, Thirza begged him to wait.

All shiny-eyed and rosy-cheeked, Libby hurried into the lamp-lit kitchen to the accompaniment of rumbling paternal wrath and her mother asking if she was not ashamed to have kept her father up until long past ten.

With rare defiance, Libby professed to see no cause for commotion. She had simply been to an interesting magic lantern show about heathen desert tribes whose bridegrooms bought their wives with camels and goats.

Articulate in anger, her father retorted that if a seventeen-stone, smelly cesspool scraper came offering a barren ewe and a stinking billy goat for Libby at that moment, he would accept quickly and expect to hand back some change.

'By all the hay on the back of your coat, I'd surmise that the parson took a collection of fodder, rather than money to help them heathen fellas. Or did it rain a shower of the grass seeds in your hair on the way back home?'

'Why, Father!' Libby blushed. 'What do you be saying? I sat by that Mrs Gritchins from over Peaspound, and all that talk of heathens paying for wives with camels made me tell her about all the things I've got put by for my bottom drawer. She showed me the lace hem she had made to put round the bottom of her petticoat thirty years ago, before she was married. She offered to lend me the same pattern and a fine silver crochet hook, so I walked back with her to get it before she changed her mind. She made me a cup of cocoa, though their kitchen was in a fair old turmoil with all them hefty sons of hers playing darts and swarming all around, all looking like peas from the same pod.'

'Doing a bit of haymaking in the kitchen, were they?' Horace's acid sarcasm was not lost on his daughter as he looked at the offending grass in Libby's hair.

'I keep trying to tell you,' she answered resignedly. 'Being so late, Mrs Gritchins asked if one of them would like to walk me home across the fields. I dropped her silver crochet hook, so we had to look for it by torchlight near their haystack down by Ducks Gutter. He came back along Foxley Bottoms with me, in case I saw the ghost.'

Desperately making mental notes in case events made future reference necessary, Thirza asked which Gritchins boy had brought her home.

Beaming happily, Libby answered, 'I'm note sure, what with all them lookalike twins and their brother, but he were a lovely lad!'

This uncertainty set warning bells ringing in Thirza's extremely anxious head. Long after Libby was safe in bed, her mother lay discussing her anxieties with Horace, in the dark. To be safe, rather than sorry, it was clearly time for Libby to wed. Ellen Gritchins could well be sizing her up for one of her sons, and since their father, Jasper, was keen to buy the mare Horace was thinking of selling, it might be advisable to drive her round their way on the following Saturday afternoon. By then Libby might well remember which son had brought her home.

Horace and Jasper Gritchins had once been 'lads of the village' together. While Horace had played the field when it came to courting, Jasper's boasted intention had always been to marry Ellen and use every letter of the alphabet as the first initial of each child they would need to name before their family was complete.

When three sets of twin boys arrived in quick succession, it seemed he might achieve his ambition, but when a singleton son was born, he appeared to run out of steam and settle for seven sons.

Watching her daughter frantically plying her crochet hook the following evening, Thirza casually remarked that the pattern did not look right. Since Horace was driving over to see if Jasper Gritchins still wanted to buy the mare on Saturday, it would be a good idea if they both went with him, then Ellen Gritchins could tell Libby where she was going wrong.

Dressed Sunday tidy, mother and daughter clambered into the two-wheeled cart on the following Saturday afternoon, Horace putting the mare through her paces as they drove into Peaspound farmyard.

Greeting them from the door, Ellen Gritchins apologized for the muddled kitchen, envying Thirza her daughter instead of having eight men to tend. Thirza responded that there was probably a young man somewhere in the background anxious to steal their precious girl away.

Jasper and Horace, having shared many youthful escapades, had no such finesse about the subject as they talked together out in the yard. Jasper came straight to the point.

'That girl of yours was here t'other evening. Why ain't a strapping great wench like her been wed?'

'She's never bothered about it, nor had Thirza and me, until one of your bright young sparks brought her home the other night, late and with hayseeds in her hair!' came Horace's sharp reply.

Inspecting the mare's hooves and fetlocks, Jasper responded cheerfully, 'Praise heaven for that! I was beginning to think my colts were only interested in darts or ferrets. She's got sound teeth then? Does she jib at hard work, or kick over the traces?'

Horace knew they were not discussing the horse. A jug of cider sealed the bargain, Jasper assembling his seven sons around the kitchen table, all looking as if they had been poured out of the same wax mould.

Smiling at Libby, he asked which one she would choose if she was so minded, Eddie who took her home, or one of the other boys.

Giggling nervously and blushing, Libby stammered, 'You are an awful tease, Mr Gritchins, I've never given any of them a thought.' She was brought to order by her father's demand that she answer 'civil like'.

Looking at the circle of likely candidates, she said she supposed it had better be Eddie, if he was the one with the big black mole on his chest.

'You crafty young devil, Eddie!' Jasper chuckled. 'If that's the way of it, there's no need for a long engagement. We could get the knot neatly tied by Christmas. In a barn of a house like this, there's no rush for them to set up home. Mother here would appreciate a bit of female help and company, and we can come mob-handed to help Horace with haymaking and harvesting, so that's all fixed.'

The two fathers shook hands on an arrangement settled to their mutual benefit.

A radiant Libby informed her parents that Eddie would walk her home after tea. As her parents rode back together, Thirza began to weep that her innocent little fledgling would soon be leaving the nest.

'About time too!' Horace answered. 'She's been twenty-eight for a couple of years, and lost a few more after her eighteenth birthday, so that even I am not sure of her proper age.'

Thirza snapped back in a rare show of impatience.

'That's simple enough. You just think back to the New Year that we were married, and take five months off that.'

Mazey Peg

Lamplight illuminated cottage windows along the village street as falling dew washed the face of the misty autumn dawn. Harassed Hilda Woodridge, bustling around her cluttered kitchen, harangued her huddle of sleep-torpid offspring to make haste and eat their bread and dripping breakfast, encouraging their progress with her sharp tongue and a few exasperated slaps.

Few village women could afford to laze in bed after six at hop harvest time, least of all Hilda, for her hop-picking money provided her steps-and-stairs, one-every-two-years family with clothing and stiff, unyielding leather boots to fend off the worst of wet winter mud. Each child was expected to pick the green hop flowers as contribution to the family exchequer.

Gran Woodridge, nearing ninety and seldom stirring her arthritic bones from the high-backed chair by Hilda's fire, was up betimes, all dressed and ready to usurp the latest toddler's right to be pushed across the orchard path to the hop field in an old canvas-seated, wooden-handled pushchair. Gran could snatch hop flowers off the vine with the best.

Beyond the village street, where the ancient yew trees shading Hag Lane denied the sun the right to shine on the timber-framed, one-storey dwelling known as Prospect Cottage, the clanging, strident bell of a battered old alarm clock made muddle-minded Peg stir in her twitching uneasy sleep. The noise became part of a frequently recurring nightmare that had dogged 'Mazey' Peg's troubled mind for more years than she cared to remember.

Sleep-bound, she imagined she still wore her nursing sister's uniform in that front-line field hospital tent in Flanders. Once again she was fighting back her nauseous fear of gunfire, and the sight of war-mutilated men. Scrambling out of bed, she saluted smartly, then hurtled a torrent of screaming invective at the clock until the alarm surrendered into silence.

Her outburst stopped as suddenly as it had started. Regaining control, reassured by her peaceful surroundings, Mazey Peg prepared for the long working day ahead, placing food and drink in a shopping basket along with a battered rusting tin that served as a first-aid box.

Children often grazed their knees and were always falling over. Few seasons passed without a minor crisis – pickers in the hoppers' huts getting scalded or burnt on their open-air cooking fires. Peg knew that most of the pickers regarded her as a crazy old coot but they all knew where to come if they were hurt.

Like Hilda Woodridge, Peg needed every penny she could earn at hop-picking time. She had no other income but a small army pension, and she was deemed to be virtually unemployable for most other indoor or agricultural work. Her disability pension of a few shillings weekly had been granted as recompense of some slight deafness in one ear, caused by a shell exploding near the hospital tent. It kept her at bare subsistence level, but she tried to be as self-sufficient as she could.

Peg had returned to civilian life, nursing among the poverty-stricken city slums for some years before the bewilderingly uncontrollable moods and horrendous nightmares started.

A medical examining board made nonsense of her claim that

her irrational behaviour had been caused by war-time experiences that were rapidly becoming the dry bones of history. Conferring together, the military medical men blandly suggested that she could well be suffering a form of hysteria sometimes found in unfulfilled females in their forties. According to their euphemistic diagnosis, she was approaching 'a funny age', and would be well advised to retreat to some quiet country spot until this cataclysmic menopausal stage of her life was safely past. Searching for seclusion, Peg found Prospect Cottage, an almost derelict dwelling surrounded by an acre of rough land. To buy it outright cost her seventy pounds.

Half a mile from the village, completely isolated, the place had a reputation for odd happenings. Witches and phantoms were supposed to haunt Hag Lane. Peg had never experienced any strange phenomena. She concluded that her own outrageous outbursts had scared any self-respecting ghosts away.

She had worked like a slave to restore the cottage, comforted that when an attack started, her foul-mouthed dementia would be witnessed by no one but herself. Thus she lived in isolation, the village inhabitants regarding her as 'mazey-yudded', a cranky middle-aged spinster, harmless enough, but best left well alone.

Restored to complete control of herself, Peg set off to work in the cold dawn light. Scuttling rabbits watched her progress across the cobweb-carpeted meadows. A flock of lapwing took flight in arrowhead formation, marking her direction towards the hop field.

Smoke swirled around half a dozen cooking fires on the open ground in front of the long row of hop huts. Shivering town-pale women, more familiar with gas rings and chip shops, shouted to each other as they brewed up their tea kettles in preparation for the start of the day. Their small, stone-floored holiday homes afforded much the same facilities that the hop-growing farmer would have given a calving cow.

The Ready family, nine in number, temporarily residing in Hut 27, were getting up in relays. Head to toe, boys and girls slept on opposite sides of the straw-filled hopsack mattresses, their parents sleeping closest to the door. Pert Polly, the eldest daughter, claimed the right to celebrate her sixteenth birthday by lingering in bed a little longer, but this concession was rejected by way of her father's prodding, smelly, sock-covered foot.

'Git up and help Ma, yer lazy pudden,' Pa grunted, still recumbent. 'Stop the nipper howling and get him changed and fed.'

The soap box, which swung suspended by knotted cords from two hooks fixed in the roof timbers, provided a makeshift, leaky cot for the youngest Ready, a moon-faced, adenoidal infant, almost two years old.

Rising, Polly flicked two earwigs from the opened condensed milk tin on a shelf above her. A four-year-old boy reluctantly relinquished possession of a huge black rubber dummy. Polly dipped it, still moist and warm, first into the milk tin, then into the nipper's gaping mouth.

Ma Ready offered a mug of tea to her supine husband. 'What's this? Boiled rat, or something?' he spluttered. Ma took one sip, then spat the offending liquid out.

'Now I know how that old faggot two doors along managed to brew her tea and cook a kipper when she only had one kettle over the fire. The old cow popped her kipper into mine. I'll scratch her eyes out!' Ma raged, marching out to do battle. Screams and exhortations rose from the row of huts, a normal beginning to a hop-picking day.

Sunrise infiltrating the eastern sky painted high clouds with crimson. As Mazey Peg joined the procession of work-bound pickers walking between the avenue of poplar trees, she was reminded of the refugees she had once encountered on another poplar-lined road.

Seeing heavily pregnant Hilda Woodridge surrounded by children and pushing a crippled old lady in a rickety-looking pushchair, Peg instinctively offered a helping hand. Although Hilda thanked her, the children's chatter petered out into awkward silence. As they passed the hop huts, Polly Ready, pushing the nipper's pram, came charging out.

Surrounded by smaller Readys, she collided with Gran's pushchair on the way. Ma Ready following, threatened her clumsy daughter with her father's belt as soon as he got up and came out to start working.

'Men!' she sighed, an exclamation that needed no explaining at all.

That morning the pickers were to start on a new hop plantation, necessitating the reallocation of each working unit, made identifiable by the huge numbered tally basket at the beginning of each row. As Mazey Peg collected her stool and picking baskets, then sat down to pick the first bines that had been cut from the strings suspended to the top wires, she realized that her row was between the Woodridge family and the Readys.

'Lord,' she prayed, 'there are children all around me. Don't let me swear.'

With so many helpers, however reluctant, both families soon moved quickly away from Peg along their hop rows. It made her efforts look puny when the tally counting man came around.

Pert Polly Ready, offering a half-empty basket, pouted the invitation: 'Would a kiss from me make this look like a full basket? It's only a matter of sixpence!'

Needing no encouragement, the lusty tally man retorted that if she cared to go behind the hedge she could earn half-a-crown far quicker than by picking hops.

Jesting, Peg chipped in with the remark: 'You would not settle for my kisses instead of hops in the tally basket, would you?'

A cold stare was her only answer, as he told Hilda Woodridge that when it came to half-baked Mazey Peg, he would rather kiss the backside of his horse.

Polly, giggling, went to join her younger brothers and sisters picking blackberries and scrumping apples through the orchard hedge. Glancing up, Peg realized what Polly was picking. She rushed forward, shouting and grabbing Polly's hands.

'I know these aren't blackberries, you daft idiot,' Polly retorted. 'They're wild grapes.'

Anxiously, Peg explained that bryony was extremely poisonous. She asked if any of the others had eaten them. A subdued Polly did not know. Peg acted fast, administering salt acquired from the hop driers at the oast and diluted with the contents of her tea bottle. Her fingers down their throats made them rewardingly sick. Ma Ready showed her appreciation by sending some of her tribe to pick into Peg's baskets, where she kept a watchful eye out for any child suffering ill effects.

Shedding the cloud blanket, the sun shone warm as any day in summer. The Ready nipper stopped crying in favour of the ubiquitous milk-dipped dummy, which fell out as he slept open-mouthed in the pram.

Ma Ready's shrill voice shattered the comparative silence,

yelling. 'Oh, Gawd! There's a wasp on the nipper's tongue. If it stings his throat it'll kill him. What shall I do?'

Within seconds the pram was surrounded by spectators, all avidly curious, but offering no help at all. Mazey Peg quietly left her picking, passing between the throng, telling them to be silent.

She took a scrumped apple from a smaller Ready lad, chewing it back to just strig and core, then went across to tug several strands away from Gran Woodridge's sparse long grey hair. Deftly tying hair to apple strig, Peg lowered it gently into the sleeping infant's open mouth, just above the wasp that crawled upon his tongue. The time seemed endless, waiting for the wasp to show interest in the apple, but the moment that it did so, Peg lifted core and wasp away.

As the pickers went back to work, Gran Woodridge hobbled over.

'Be it true that a good soul like you be sometimes troubled by the devil? You wants to go to the belfry when church bells be ringing. Church bells were first made to drive evilness away!'

At that moment a picker-turned-poacher fired a shotgun in the nearby orchard. Peg felt the familiar wave of apprehension flow over her and heard her own voice shouting, hideous and obscene. She was banished from the hop field at once.

Word of Peg's outburst spread through the village and the townee pickers' encampment, most tales being further embroidered as they were told.

Some righteous folk talked of demonic forces, while there were those in favour of literally driving out the strange woman who had moved into Prospect Cottage with her airs and graces. The contents of her cesspool mind had been revealed by her own tongue.

Common sense prevailed, the more level-headed majority believing that while Mazey Peg had proved to be an evil-tongued misfit, she had harmed no one. She was best left to her own devices. Hilda Woodridge believed Peg's outburst stemmed from the fact that she had been left on the matrimonial shelf. There was nothing like having a husband and a parcel of kids to bring a woman's mind down to earth.

Hop picking ended. Peg became more reclusive, knowing that she had become the village bogey man, with parents actually threatening recalcitrant children that they would be sent down Hag Lane to Mazey Peg if they misbehaved.

With the days getting colder as they grew shorter, Peg made frequent firewood-gathering expeditions along the nearby woodland tracks. Unknown to Peg one October Saturday morning, weekend guests from The Hall were preparing for 'Lordy's' first pheasant shoot of the season. As she was returning home with the sack of dead wood on her back, the guns were taking station along the field hedge at the end of the lane in readiness for the village men and boy beaters to drive the birds towards them. As Peg turned the corner she heard the shout 'Pheasant Up', and the subsequent blasts of a double-barrelled shotgun fired less than twenty yards away.

The sack on her back became the seventeen-year-old soldier she had once carried from a shelled field hospital, crying for his mother, with his arm and half his face blown away. Her screaming brought the sporting gentleman running towards her, thinking that by some terrible mischance he had shot her. The under-gamekeeper, acting as his gun loader, reassured him that this was only Mazey Peg, a daft-headed female given to sudden outbursts of swearing that would make a regimental sergeant major blush for shame.

'Don't fret yourself, sir. She's acted weird ever since she came here, carrying her rusty old tin case full of bandages and suchlike about all the time. Not so long ago she put the fear of the devil in some women out in the hop fields, getting them to make their kids drink tea with salt in it because she swore they had eaten poison berries. She even shoved her finger down their throats to make them sick, poor little blighters. 'Twas all a fuss about nothing. None of them took poorly or died. I believe she gets some sort of pension from the government, or a hospital or something. Hereabouts us give her a wide berth.'

The middle-aged sportsman handed his gun to his loader somewhat angrily.

'Wide berth be damned! I'm a doctor. As a wartime major in the Royal Army Medical Corp, I saw enough patients to recognize shell shock. I worked alongside young nurses who had probably encountered nothing more violent than the Hunt Ball, or the Tennis Club mixed doubles final, until they were sent to the base field hospitals in France and Belgium. Those girls dealt

efficiently with injuries no human being should endure, uncom-
plaining, looking neat and cheerful for their patients, working
until they dropped. You say she always carries a battered metal
first-aid box?'

As the under-gamekeeper nodded, the Major, late of the
RAMC, turned to Peg and bellowed: 'Sister! Remember what
you are!'

Peg's shouting stopped immediately. Her bent and shaking
frame straightened up as she saluted and answered: 'Sir!'

Conducting a perfectly lucid conversation, they established
that they had once both served in the same field hospital in
France at varying times during the Great War. Sending his
loader out of eavesdropping distance, the Major evinced the
story of Peg's post-war trauma. The increasingly horrific nightmares left her shouting uncontrollably, forcing her to give up
nursing and hide herself away in the solitude of the cottage in
Hag Lane.

'Something must and will be done to help you. That I
promise.'

He certainly kept his word. On the following Monday morning, Perce, the village postman, reported seeing Mazey Peg,
tidy-dressed and sitting beside the chauffeur in the blue Daimler
limousine belonging to one of Lordy's shooting friends.

Peg was eventually admitted to a famous military hospital
where X-rays revealed that a fragment of her hairline-cracked
skull had been pressing on her brain ever since she was knocked
flat by the shell blast in that wartime front-line hospital. Subsequent surgery to relieve this and restore her to normality
proved less than successful. Gone were the ghosts of a nightmare
war, for she now lay unaware of the world around her. Growing
ever weaker, she survived until the following September when
the village was busy with the hop harvest. Word went round the
hop field that Mazey Peg had passed on. Ma Ready had mar-
shalled her tribe from the hop huts to start picking bines a few
rows away from where Hilda Woodridge and the indomitable
Gran were snatching off hops nineteen to the dozen.

Ma called across to Hilda for confirmation of Peg's passing, expressing her regret: 'Say what you like, Mazey Peg might have
sworn like a trooper when she was upset, but she knew what to
do when that wasp was in my Raymond's mouth. Daft as she was,
she likely saved his life. God rest her soul.'

Gran chimed in: 'She was helpful to me and my poor feet last hopping when Hilda was too close to her time to bend down and do my nails. That dinner time when you all cleared off to get your share of the eating apples that farmer couldn't sell, she stayed back with me and took some sharp clippers and a file out of that battered old tin box she always carried, and eased my feet a treat. I never had nothing against her. Poor soul couldn't help being daft.'

Hilda picked her bine in silence for a few moments.

'Mazey Peg weren't really daft,' she admitted. 'My niece Phylis sometimes helps wait at table up at The Hall. She heard His Nibs and Her Ladyship discussing a Sister Margaret for some time before she realized they were talking about Mazey Peg. They called her an unsung heroine, deserving a medal from the King. How was we to know she had been injured nursing front-line troops in the battlefields, and been walking around with a head like a cracked egg? We couldn't be knowing that the rusty old tin box she used when kids cut themselves and needed bandaging out in the hop fields, was the first-aid case she carried all through the war. It's not our fault if she acted like she was a daft-yudded female with old maid's disease, is it? Nobody told us!'

'S'pose not!' Ma Ready replied quietly.

An unusually subdued atmosphere prevailed in the hop field all morning. A chill breeze sighed among the hop bines as a bank of cloud covered the face of the sun as if to hide its shame.

The Hope and Anchor

With sea birds and sheep as neighbours and the nearest house almost a mile away, the Hope and Anchor beer-house down by Marsh Side jetty would have seemed the ideal place to lose a fortune fast. Nevertheless, the brewery drayman drove his team of Clydesdales out across the marsh track regularly each week, delivering more beer than the village pubs would hope to sell in a dry, hot, harvesting month.

The brown-sailed coastal barges, which carried cargoes of timber and grain up Town Creek waterway, could only navigate the narrow, twisting, deep-water channel on the rising tide. If they reached the estuary near low water, they anchored off Marsh Side jetty and took on liquid refreshment while they waited for the tide to turn.

In the 1930s, the licensee was a formidable old woman who in her time had been known to remove forcibly argumentative or drunken bargees from the establishment and pitch them off the jetty into the black sea mud. Years of cold stone floors and marsh damp eventually made her bed-bound, her daughter, Polly, taking over the running of the place.

Any seafaring man who 'looked sideways' in her direction was warned off. Polly had had a sweetheart ever since her school days, and if by the 1930s Steve had spent at least thirty-five years unsuccessfully popping the question, age did not wither his affection. 'Old Poll' couldn't wed and leave her mother. He too had the responsibility of taking care of a senile old Dad.

Each Saturday when his work was finished, Steve would polish his cycle clips, then pedal off across the marsh to spend an hour with his loved one. Summer, winter, heat wave, flood or snow-drifts, he never went without two posies of flowers. One for Poll and one for 'the old gal'.

The winter of 1939 was bitterly cold. By that Christmas, Poll's mother and Steve's old Dad had gone to their last rest. The lovers regarded any question of their getting married as unseemly for a few mourning months. By that time our countryside was sheltering survivors of Dunkirk. Poll's reaction was that this was no time to get wed. While she was busy gallivanting up the aisle, the Germans could well be sailing up Town Creek.

So Steve continued his routine of Saturday courting, and Poll kept lonely watch for invaders, with a loaded shotgun behind her bar 'just in case'.

Steve became a part-time fireman. In his off-duty hours he helped us on the land. We welcomed his company that summer, for while we harvested our crops, the Battle of Britain was being fought above our heads. We were carrying wheat in Starve Crow Field one morning, Dad and Steve pitching sheaves while I loaded the waggon. Jim, the chestnut horse, was in the shafts, Smudge, the black mongrel dog who imagined she was my shadow, trotting along behind.

The weather looked uncertain. We had taken tarpaulin covers down to the field to sheet up the waggons as we loaded them, but our four-footed friends had other ideas. Smudge was the first to become apprehensive, emitting the sharp staccato barks she made when something made her uneasy, then, still yapping as if asking me to follow, she headed off across the field for home. Jim too became restless, jerking the waggon, refusing to stand still while the men were loading, and almost pitching me off the top of the load.

He was normally the most reasonable of horses, but without any warning he took off, running the nearside wheels of the waggon over the new tarpaulins in his headlong flight towards the closed field gate. Dad and Steve decided that half a load in the barn was better than an overturned waggon and a crippled loader. Jim, wet with sweat, ears laid back and twitching, stood trembling as Steve and Dad caught up with us.

Steve reckoned that a swarm of hornets must be flying around to bother both dog and horse. In a way he was right, for no sooner had we got the load in through the high barn doorway, than all hell broke loose overhead. We knew that Spitfires and Hurricanes frequently patrolled above us, so much so that we used to count them heading coastwards, then anxiously count them home. This time two 'Hurrys' were mixing it with a gaggle of Messerschmitt fighters that were escorting a squadron of Heinkel bombers.

My mother, who had run across from the house to find out why we had returned so early, stood with her hands clasped, praying as the fighters screamed to their funeral pyres and a bomber disintegrated with an ear-splitting explosion.

'Dear God, they are all some mothers' sons.'

We carried on unloading the wheat sheaves into the barn bays, then tentatively led Jim and the waggon out across the yard towards Starve Crow Field again. He walked off quite happily. With her tail waggling like a flag behind her, Smudge trotted along too. When we got out into the field, we realized how lucky we had been that Jim made us leave it, for it was littered with jagged metal.

Steve regarded the pock-marked heaps of earth in the stubble.

'Strewth, Harry, looks like them old rabbits have been summat busy again.' Finding the tarpaulin cover we had left was now riddled with bullet holes, Steve held up one corner and muttered, 'Mice?'

A column of black smoke still curled skywards, and from my vantage point on top of the load I could see that it was not far from the Hope and Anchor across the marsh. We heard two blasts of gunfire.

'That's Poll's old double-barrelled shotgun,' Steve said anxiously, hurrying off to investigate.

It was late afternoon when he reappeared, pink-eared and blushing. Anxiously we asked about old Poll.

'Never seen nothing like it,' said Steve, chuckling.

'When I gets over to the Hope and Anchor, there's old Poll standing guard with her shotgun outside the privy door. "What you got in there then, Poll?" I asks her. "A Nasty," her says. "He landed out on the mud bank and comes walking up the jetty large as life. He keeps on hollering, but it don't make no difference. I've shut him in the privy and there he stays."'

Steve had soldiered in Germany in 1919 and thought he'd know a Nazi if he met one. Taking possession of the shotgun, he unbarred the privy door. A very irate mud-plastered young man stepped out. Steve tried out a few words of his German. No response. Whatever his nationality, the aviator was not British. His uniform was completely different. Steve knew that some French and Polish flyers were now serving with the RAF.

'De Gaulle' aroused no enthusiasm in the disgruntled young man, so Steve tried out the only two Polish words he knew, 'Warsaw' and 'Paderewski'.

The effect was instant and dramatic, Steve collecting a muddy kiss on both cheeks. Poll said she had no idea that he was a gifted linguist. It all sounded double Dutch to her.

An air-sea rescue launch collected the Polish flyer from Marsh Side jetty and Steve returned to work.

'Poor old Poll. All that excitement must have made her come all over of a flutter, because after all these years, I'm blowed if her didn't pucker up her lips and kiss me fair and square. Reckon if I play my cards right I'll have her marching up the aisle alongside me, time this war is done. Don't do to rush old Poll, though. I could end up like those old bargees that used to torment her mother, flat on my back in Marsh Side mud.'

The Fund Raisers

The village Gala had proved to be remarkably successful, the weather fine, the entrance money takings mounting up. In the field events our home tug-of-war team had defied all comers, shrugging off the disgruntled comments of defeated opponents who complained that our village had always been noted for breeding more brawn than brains.

Competitors from as far afield as Foxley, Lockley, Ducks Gutter, and Tylers End took part in the 'Four Steeples' twelve-mile running race, but Slippy Springer, who had learned to travel fast and rely on his turn of speed to outpace poacher-hunting estate gamekeepers, was over the finishing line and downing a victory pint of cider before his nearest rival staggered into view.

From the moment Her Ladyship declared the show open, old Henry Drapper had stayed in the garden produce tent proudly displaying his enormous pair of prize-winning onions, while those beholding Charlie Chappell's champion marrow were unanimous that when it came to the length and circumference of his exhibit, nothing to match it had been raised in local parts for years.

The goods on the sewing bee stall had dwindled to a few felt egg cosies, embroidered chair backs and knitted kneecap warmers, while the cake stall trestle was a white-sheet-covered wilderness with just a few overcooked rock cakes remaining unsold.

The washstand ewers, which had been filled to the brim with powdery concentrated lemonade, were now empty wasp-haunted vessels, while Miss Fountwater's home-made ice cream was reduced to a few runny scoops, liquifying and dripping from soft, soggy cones.

The village school pupils' display of country dancing, singing and recitation passed off happily, overlooking the embarrassingly unfortunate moment when the young lady soloist who stood chirruping 'Cherry Ripe', suddenly developed an acute attack of stage fright and wet her drawers. A wave of sympathy encouraged the stolid little lad who bravely started to recite 'The boy stood on the burning deck, whence all but he had fled'. Every ex-pupil present had endured countless hours learning the same epic poem, but try as we would to prompt him, no one could remember how the following line ran.

The smartly uniformed City Silver Band had sweated their way through 'The Washington Post', 'Colonel Bogey', 'Blaze Away', 'Bells Across the Meadow' and 'Sanctuary of the Heart'. Behind the committee tent, the cheerful show officials were partaking of celebratory mugs of rough farm cider when a small boy came scurrying importantly towards them, destroying their calm.

''Ere!' he panted. 'Mr Walls over at the gate have sent me urgent like, to say His Nibs's Daimler car be coming down the lane with Her Ladyship on board.'

'What the 'ell can she want?' Proddy Price grumbled. 'She's done her speechifying, spent her usual two quid round the stalls and cadged cuttings and buds from all the best plants in the show, so why has she come back now?'

Albert Parsley being more temperate in his manner and reactions, remarked that as patroness of the show, Her Ladyship was within her rights to come back and see how they were faring financially. As treasurer, he would be happy to inform her that the takings were a vast improvement on the previous year.

'Good on you!' Proddy answered. 'Tell the pompous old trout the glad tidings quick Albert, then with any luck, perhaps she will go.'

Deferentially approaching the Daimler as it sighed across the grass, Albert informed Her Ladyship of the increased profits as she alighted from the car.

'Absolutely top hole! Frightfully well done,' she remarked, turning away from Albert and heading for the rug-covered beer crates that had served as a rostrum for the conductor of the City Silver Band. Cutting short his 'Tales from the Vienna Woods', she elbowed him out of her way, demanding a rallying drum roll and a blast on the cornet.

'Gather round everyone,' she beckoned imperiously. 'Yes, I do mean everyone!' Satisfied that she had the undivided attention of her listeners, she made her announcement: 'The events of today have proved that as a parish you are capable of showing interest in the world in which you live. Just as I afford your village show my patronage, so do my charitable duties extend to other more important institutions and events. As you may know, I am a governor of the Town Cottage Hospital. Watching your efforts today made me realize how little this community contributes to so worthy a cause. Most of you put a penny per person per week into the hospital collecting box with which each household is supplied, but this is not nearly sufficient. Several of you owe the Cottage Hospital your lives.'

Imagining that Her Ladyship's pause for breath meant that she was waiting for volunteers to relate their surgical experience, old Dubber Walls began to describe the symptoms of his extremely embarrassing personal problems, until a trip to the hospital put his waterworks right. Another parishioner volunteered to pop home and fetch the gall stones that had made life a misery before her operation, but now had pride of place in a glass-stoppered jar on her front room mantelshelf.

Ignoring mundane medical matters, Her Ladyship imperiously held up her hand for silence.

'All proceeds of this year's Town Carnival Parade are to go to the Cottage Hospital. I look to you to offer more support to this effort beyond just standing with your mouths open watching it pass by. I shall expect to see at least two tableau floats from this village, not to mention the decorated bicycles, the prettiest perambulator, and the pedestrian fancy-dress classes. From my position with the mayoral party I will watch out for participants in the procession from this village, and for nonparticipants throwing coins along the route. Show some life and initiative. You would do well to remember that those who show no interest in supporting other people's worthy causes cannot expect influential persons to show concern for their welfare in return. Come now! Other villages select their beauty queens. Surely we can find a few decent-looking fillies who would come forward. I am making this a personal issue. This village must dispel its insular reputation. I am now asking for volunteer organizers to step forward.'

Among the hastily retreating crowd, Proddy Price asked Albert what insular meant.

Albert considered the question for a moment, then replied, 'It's something to do with electricals, I reckon, like not getting struck by lightning in a thunderstorm.'

'No, it ain't,' Tom Grommett argued. 'It's what they treat sugar diabetes with.'

The large proportion of the village population whose livelihoods were in some measure dependent on Lordy's estates, mulled over Her Ladyship's words, aware of the threatening implications underlying her remarks.

With the last of the day's events ended, the stalwarts cleaning up the field considered the situation, agreeing that it was better to placate Her Ladyship's little whims and notions than to risk their jobs. The blacksmith was sure his wife would be willing to organize one entry for the procession, providing suitable transport could be found. Tom Grommett eagerly offered to dress up as the Sheik of Araby so long as he could ride in the parade in close proximity to seven or eight scantily clad members of his harem, but his buxom, tightly corseted wife soon killed Tom's fantasy stone dead.

After no other contestants could be cajoled into coming forward, Pansy Troop was persuaded to take off her thick-lensed glasses and accept the bead and silver wire crown as our village beauty queen. The throne that was built on a farm cart looked somewhat incongruous and pretentious, so ex-seaman Bunting

Dawes rigged up a garlanded swing held in place by guy ropes. It seemed a novel invention at the time. Pansy looked as decorative as an Easter egg in a shimmery gold and purple borrowed bridesmaid's gown.

The Women's Institute chose Florence Nightingale as their inspiration. Under the dynamic, not to say dictorial direction of Parson's sister, the back of the fruit farm lorry was transformed into a war in Scutari Military Hospital, complete with iron bedstead, army blankets, and strips of sheeting bandage liberally bespattered with red paint.

Dressed in her long grey shirt, starched cap and nurse's apron, Parson's formidable sister held her lamp aloft like a homing beacon. One glaring, tight-lipped glance was enough to stifle any frivolity from the pair of recumbent wounded soldiers, and we few who had been persuaded to dress up as Miss Nightingale's helpers.

She grew more tense and irritable as we assembled for the judging at the start of the procession, and as I gave a dying hero a cup of something that was not water, he groaned, 'I do reckon that if them Women's Institutes had been in the Thin Red Line at the Battle of Balaclava, its end would have been a different tale.'

Due to a rare outbreak of punctuality, our float arrived early enough to be placed in the forefront of the procession, right behind the town fire engine and the Sea Scouts' Drum and Fife Band. As we moved off along a narrow road to turn into the main thoroughfare leading to the High Street, the lorry began to misfire, jerk and judder, making protesting grinding noises in its internal workings before it rolled to a halt. We stood immobile, completely blocking the narrow street, watching the fire engine and the Sea Scouts' Band disappear into the distance, while the rest of the procession came to a traffic-jammed halt behind.

Some coarser elements in the following float made some very rude and ribald gestures, one loud-mouthed joker offering Parson's sister advice: 'Go on then, missus! Rub that ruddy lamp!'

It needed more than a magic lamp to free a jammed gearbox. The rest of the procession was diverted in through the back gate of the brewery and out through the front. Carried away by the cheering, clapping onlookers, short-sighted Pansy became so excited and disorientated with her swinging, that she came over all faint and seasick, falling off backwards as the transport suddenly stopped to negotiate the narrow turning into the main road from the brewer's yard, thus holding up the procession yet again.

On hearing of Pansy's predicament, Florence Nightingale hastily evacuated her patients, nurses and blood-red painted bandages from the broken down lorry, commandeering Pansy's paper-flower-bedecked farm waggon. We collected many odd glances along with the thrown pennies as we paraded round the town.

Tom Grommett had borrowed Dairyman Dave's milk float, transforming it into a Roman chariot. He drove Dave's placid old pony, Lightning, with a flourish, standing on the back step all swathed round in a white sheet, with a plumed and polished copper coal scuttle on his head and his plump wife dressed as an unlikely-looking slave by his side.

Few onlookers were able to appreciate his efforts. Lightning knew only one way through the town streets, and that was the route of his early morning milk round. Tom Grommett could do nothing to dissuade him from following his set routine, stopping at every customer's house along the way.

If our carnival efforts had earned little praise and no prizes, we rode homeward in the back of the sick-engined fruit farm lorry content that we had done our best to raise funds for the Cottage Hospital. We had certainly patronized it that evening, calling in on the way home to enquire after Pansy, who had been admitted with suspected concussion and had to stay there overnight.

Getting a Bit of Help

Abigail put aside the soapy washboard to dry her work-roughened hands on a hessian 'scrubbing apron' that encompassed her bulky figure like a slackly filled chaff sack.

Having fed dry faggot wood to the copper fire, she emerged from the steamy candlelit wash house to pad purposefully across the damp and rather slippery cobbles of the yard.

A pair of half-wild farm cats disputing ownership of a partially eaten rat on the back doorstep disregarded her approach until she stumbled over them. Abandoning their booty, they scuttled off like shadows, merging with the early morning darkness that enshrouded the run-down old buildings around the perimeter of the yard.

Scolding at life in general, Abigail entered the low raftered back kitchen to find a draught-driven flame flaring up in the soot-blackened glass chimney of the oil lamp on the table. Its disinterested murky light intensified the damp-patched drab discomfort of the stone-floored room.

'Drat and darn it!' Abigail muttered, knowing that cleaning the lamp and trimming the wick would now be an additional task to perform in the long and busy day ahead. A stiff-boned old sheepdog shuffled away from the hearthrug to take cowering refuge under the kitchen table as his mistress attempted to rake the dead ashes in the kitchen stove into some semblance of life. Tick-tocking its way to eternity, an old moon-faced clock chimed the third quarter of the hour.

'What be you in such a rush for when I am so busy?' Abigail inquired, as if she expected the mechanism to answer back. 'Lord Almighty! I clean forgot that them two lazy lummocks are still laying in bed!'

She hurried into a narrow hallway that smelled of dry rot and mouldering lino, shouting up into the void of darkness above the staircase.

'Arthur! Reggie! Just you stir yourselves, you lay-a-bed lumps! 'Tis past a quarter to six already! I've been up since half-past four and have a copperload of washing boiled, rinsed and ready for mangling, while you two idle werts are stuck up there as if your father had nailed your shirt-tails to the bed. He's been up and around the stock for the last hour, and is likely to take his belt to the pair of you if you are not downstairs and stirring your stumps when he comes in. Shift yourselves now, or I'll get my copper stick to you.'

For all that Abigail's boys were past thirty, they recognized the fact that this was no idle threat. Abigail heard the sagging springs of an old bedstead clanking overhead as a sleep-slurred voice called down.

'What's the matter, Ma? If this be Monday washday then I've slept clean through Friday, Saturday, and changing my shirt for Sunday.'

'With Michaelmas Fair tomorrow and all them stock sales and farm auctions next week, the washing that is not done today will wait a fortnight!' Abigail snapped in answer. 'Just get down here and draw up some more water from the well!'

Returning to the kitchen, she found the fire still sulkily smouldering under the smoke-grimed kettle.

The puffing leather hand bellows failed to inspire the fire into activity, so she shook a handful of sugar over the half-burned sticks to ignite them, hoping her husband would not detect such wastefulness.

Scratcher's eyes, ears and nose missed little when it came to thrift. Lean and darting in his movements, he came in through the back door, grumbling at his wife.

'If you can afford to feed the fire with toffee, missus, you can take a cut in your housekeeping. It's a poor lookout for a working man when there's no sign of breakfast or a cup of tea an hour after he's risen. I've left the milk in the calving shed. Don't let it cool before you bucket feed them bobby calves I bought you. By the way, the copper is boiling over. It's like a devil's Sabbath with all the smoke and steam coming from the wash house. You should keep an eye on your work and not dart about. When do you reckon you'll get a chance to crate up them fattening cockerels to sell at the fair market, if you don't do it this morning?'

Busily cutting hunks of bread and dripping, Abigail made no answer until her two sons ambled into the kitchen to stand waiting for her to pour them mugs of tea.

'I should have been born with a few extra pairs of hands,' she grumbled, 'for there's too much work for the pair I have now!'

'Then you'd have been a fairground freak and it's likely Dad wouldn't have married you!' Arthur retorted.

'I dare not dwell on the prospect like that!' Abigail snapped sarcastically. But her mind did dwell on the perpetual grind and poverty of affection that summarized her marriage from the start.

Husband Thomas had gained the appropriate nickname of Scratcher as a youth, because he had sought no other pastime but earning extra shillings while all the other as yet unshaven lads of his own age were apple scrumping, kicking a football around, or whistling after girls.

Scratcher's propensity for work rated him as a 'good prospect' in the estimation of Abigail's domineering parents, who at that time seemed anxious to get their only child safely married and off their hands.

In their estimation, a chap with a 'bit put by' was someone to be actively encouraged, for all that his courtship technique had as much warmth and affection in approach as he would have extended to his search for a comfortable hard-wearing pair of new heavy working boots at the cheapest knockdown price.

Abigail then seventeen and ignorant of the facts of life, was browbeaten into believing that Scratcher's offhand, brusque attitude proved his decency. Father knew best about such matters. Her mother hinted that there would be a miraculous alteration in Scratcher's manner as soon as his wedding ring was on Abigail's finger. New depths of affection would emerge. Undoubtedly he was being a gentleman and 'holding himself back' until after he was decently married. Opportunity did not knock twice. Abigail must be grateful that so hard-working a chap had come along to ask her father's permission. It had always been a woman's lot to bear with the ways of men; Abigail must learn to accept it.

That had been the total sum of motherly prenuptial advice offered to a girl who had previously never been allowed to go to choir practice unescorted.

Being somewhat unsociable and awkward in front of strangers, Abigail's bridegroom had not been introduced to her relatives until after the wedding ceremony. Her maternal grandmother, then in her eighties, did not like what she saw. Calling Abigail aside, the frail little soul whispered that she needed to talk somewhere that they would not be overheard. For the benefit of those around them, she adopted the bad-tempered attitude of a demanding old lady.

'Bride you may be, young Abi, but I still needs your help to go down the garden path to the privy, my girl.'

In these insalubrious surroundings, Abigail's grandmother had delved under multitudinous layers of flannel underclothing to bring out a small wash-leather, drawstring bag that had hung round her neck on a long leather thong. She handed this to Abigail, her anxiety written plain on her face.

'You have taken on nought but grief and toil with that one, my Abi. Be them daft beggars blind not to see what they have got you hitched up with. All that talk about finding you a hard-working husband who will make sure he is never penniless! He's the kind that would whip a willing horse till it dropped. You too, if I'm not mistaken, so here's a little bit of insurance, girl. Go on open it!'

Abigail untied the worn wash-leather purse and counted out five golden sovereigns. She tried to hand them back, saying that she could not possibly take such a gift from her grandmother, her voice unsteady with emotion for this one person in the world that had ever shown her real humanity and love. Her Gran said sharply that they had no time to stand snivelling like a couple of frightened children. She had something to say and Abigail must listen carefully and pay good heed to her advice.

'My own mother gave me those five coins on the day I was wed, making me promise that I would never even think of spending any of them until the day I believed myself to be without help or hope. I was lucky, Abi. I didn't need to.

'When your mother married your know-all father, they were so smug and self-sufficient that my little wash-leather bag would have gone to the grave with me rather than let those precious coins fall into their grasping hands. Hide it safe. Tell no one in the world about it. Save secretly to make a nest egg, even if you can only find three farthings to take to the post office each week. Although you have promised to stay married until you die, there might come a day when you will be thankful for that little bit of independence. Your man is cold stone through and through. I doubt if you will even warm the edges. Now we'll toddle back down the path and I'll act the helpless old woman who takes half an hour to get her drawers pulled down and up again. We'll have to go back to the celebrations, but God knows that there will be little reason for anyone to rejoice.'

Abigail had been young and foolish enough to doubt Gran's assessment of Scratcher, but she took the advice the old lady had offered, hiding the wash-leather bag and starting a Post Office Savings Account that seldom increased by much more than sixpence a week down through the years.

Gran died in her sleep a few weeks after the wedding. Any illusions concerning her husband's affections were irrevocably shattered just ten months after her wedding on that August night before her twin sons were born. Tired from barley mowing the previous day, Scratcher refused to get up and summon the nurse when Abigail's labour started. He rose at his usual time, fed his stock, milked his cows, then went to fetch the midwife. Consequently Abigail delivered first-born Arthur herself. The nurse's timely arrival saved Reggie's life. Scratcher's greeting when he saw his sons for the first time was less than loving.

'Why the devil did you have to choose harvest time to litter down? You can't lay abed with me still waiting for my dinner! The harvest gang can't work on empty bellies. I can't act lady's maid and do your work as well as my own!'

She was up and working normally within two days of her twins' birth, and from that time on she shared Scratcher's toil and troubles but never his bed.

There had been times when Abigail longed to hear a word of appreciation or affection, but it had never been forthcoming. To some extent, his attitude that she was a family workhorse influenced the two boys, who grew up to regard her in much the same way. She knew that she would never now be able to change the situation that had become the set pattern of her family life. Perhaps it was as well that there was always more than enough work to occupy her mind as well as her hands.

Certainly this was no time to remind Scratcher that they had been yoked together in marriage for thirty-two years on that autumn day. Instead she reminded Arthur and Reggie of their promise to draw water from the well and fetch faggot wood to stoke the copper fire before they started work in the fields.

Her husband answered sharply: 'They ain't skivvies, missus! You've kept us hanging about for breakfast for so long, we're late starting as it is!'

Carrying water pails and firewood for the copper, Abigail kept her thoughts to herself.

Four hungry baby calves were bellowing for her attention, their muzzles soft and warm as they nuzzled around her while she fed them warm milk from a pail. Their vulnerability only served to emphasize the burden of work that lay on her shoulders, with no foreseeable hope of relief. Years before when 'women's troubles' had beset her, she tentatively employed a young girl to help her, but Scratcher sent her packing within hours, wanting no dizzy females to eat their heads off and taunt his sons around the place.

This attitude prevailed when the boys had plucked up enough courage to start walking out with two sisters who had worked for an elderly lady for some years. Their employer complained that she would allow no one to pester her servants. This suited Scratcher, his belt and several doses of opening medicine 'doctoring' their food soon made his sons settle down.

Those two plain women still lived in the house their employer had bequeathed to them in her will. They smiled coyly whenever Abigail saw them, as if they might still retain affection for her slow lumpkin sons.

As she turned the handle of the heavy-rollered mangle, an idea formed in her mind. It seemed inspirational, yet it was so simple a solution, she wondered why she had not thought of it before. Hurrying into the kitchen, she stirred through the dresser drawer to find pen and paper, then sat down to write.

Dear Misses. My sons Arthur and Reggie want to meet you at the Michaelmas Fair tomorrow at eleven o'clock in the town square. They be shy at stating their business, but be steady workers. Yours, etc. . . .

Abigail gave her missive to the postman. Work went more easily after that.

On this annual day of freedom from the daily grind, Abigail wore her blue serge costume and straw hat that had served as 'best clothes' for the last twelve years, her shape secured in the constricting whale-boned corset that stayed in her bedroom cupboard for most other days of the year.

Shaved, tidy and considerably smarter in appearance than usual, Scratcher and the boys set off for town in the farm waggon, Abigail riding encumbered around with chicken crates, fruit, vegetables and the various other items Scratcher intended to sell.

Knowing that Scratcher resented her presence in the market hall when their stock was being auctioned, Abigail was set to enjoy a precious few hours of freedom, having first ensured that her sons were in the right place at the right time to meet up with the husband-hungry sisters. She watched all four standing giggling and gawking for a few moments before they paired off and headed in the general direction of the amusement stalls.

Thankful that she had given Arthur and Reggie a ten-shilling note each as extra spending money, she felt the same sense of satisfaction to be gained when a bit of yeast is added to flour and water, and a heavy mass of stodgy dough begins to rise. Hopefully there would soon be two pairs of willing hands to ease her burden of hard work, if the sisters were really desperate enough to want her stolid sons as husbands, and the twins were not too slow to grab their chance.

After wandering round the market stalls for a while, Abigail felt hungry, but Scratcher disapproved of cafés and shop-bought 'vittals', demanding that none of his family wasted good money on such dangerous, expensive, chemically treated muck.

Instead, Abigail had always brought a basket of the kind of home-made pasties she baked for Scratcher's once-a-fortnight trips to town on market day, Scratcher proudly boasting that he had never wasted money in a restaurant in his life.

Maybe the dim prospect that her sons might at long last be brave enough to defy their father and take the first tottering steps towards matrimony made her feel defiant of Scratcher's parsimonious restrictions. She decided to spend a shilling on cream cakes and a pot of tea at the Cavena Café. She had often glanced through their front windows at the spotless starched tablecloths, with little vases of real flowers on them, and the pretty rosebud patterning of their china crockery.

Entering through the swing doors resolutely, she walked into a warm atmosphere softly lit by wall lamps with fluted pink shades. High-backed settles transformed each table into an individual enclave where customers could sit undisturbed by the activity of a café busy with the rush of Michaelmas Fair-goers.

Abigail chose to sit at an empty table in the shadowy far corner of the restaurant, wishing to enjoy this rare moment of luxury undisturbed as she leaned back in the velvet-covered, pew-like seat. In apologizing for the delay in serving her, a friendly waitress explained that shortage of staff meant that those on duty were rushed off their feet. Glad to stop a moment to ease her throbbing bunion from the pressure of her shoe, the waitress continued to bemoan her lot.

'I can't understand that in a time of unemployment our manager can't get reliable staff, and this is a decent fair firm to work for. It is the same in other branches, even down along the coast.'

Abigail savoured every mouthful of her cream pastries until she recognized a familiar voice amid the general burble of conversation. She sat statue still, unashamedly eavesdropping on the unseen customers in the enclave behind her. Scratcher was in earnest conversation with a female companion who had obvious reason to complain.

'Being together for a couple of hours once a fortnight is not good enough, Thomas. We're neither of us getting any younger, and you've been courting me this past twenty years. Don't think

I'm complaining, love. You are so generous with your money, and it must be hell to be tied to a disagreeable invalid all this time.'

Too stunned to move momentarily, Abigail heard Scratcher saying words he had never spoken to her, even when they were first wed. She rose and went round to the next table, ready to confront him.

'Ah!' he said, somewhat disconcerted. 'This lady is my school-mate's widow. She has just been offering to come and help out. There is so much to do around the house, and she needs somewhere to live.'

'I'm sure she would be very welcome,' Abigail smiled angelically. 'I don't know how you have managed to cope with your invalid wife for so long.'

A podgy little woman with frizzy permed hair beamed up at her, Scratcher meanwhile sitting open-mouthed and lost for words.

'Good luck then!' Abigail said, walking away with her head held high, sensing her own freedom. In her fifty years she had known little of life but hard work, heartache and rejection. A few moments of conversation with the café manager at the cash desk confirmed the prospect of immediate employment at another branch. Her Gran-inspired emergency fund and the unexpected small nest egg legacy from her mother would tide her over nicely.

There seemed nothing strange in riding along the coast road in a lumbering bus, without luggage or regret that she had simply walked away from the thousand and one daily tasks around her loveless marital home. There would soon be plenty of helping hands there, without her own. Filled with a great sense of relief, freedom and confidence in her own future, Abigail now knew why the old lady who had been the only one to have ever shown understanding or affection had given her so strange a wedding gift.

She rode towards the future clutching Gran's five gold sovereigns in their wash-leather bag.

The Pump and Shovel Volunteers

At a time when our corner of the country seemed destined to bear the brunt of invasion and an increasing number of hit-and-run raids were tuning up for the prelude to the Battle of Britain in the skies above our heads, word went round of a hastily arranged meeting that everyone in the village would do well to attend. A notice outside the Post Office Stores doubly underlined the subject of the meeting: top priority Civil Defence matters of vital importance to all civilians. Within an hour of this notice being posted up, housewives collecting a free sample of gossip along with their grocery rations were convinced there was truth and substance in the rumour that our village was to become part of an extended military area, with all civilians evacuated and the place booby-trapped with mines.

Agricultural men, who set the world to rights on Saturday afternoons as they sat along the forge yard wall waiting for an old shepherd to ply sheep shears and horse clippers around their heads for a 'Shup Special' fourpenny haircut, were convinced that we were to be given last-minute instructions by chinless Ministry officials from 'up country' telling us what to do when invasion came.

Farmer Frank Robbins viewed the possibility of a 'Chins Up. Think of England' pep talk with resentment.

'No jumped-up townee in a braided hat is going to tell me how to act when I see old Hitler and his Nasties heading up over Lockley Hill! I've sorted that one out already. I'll turn all the livestock loose to fend for themselves, then I'll empty bags of lime all over the vegetables in the garden and the oats and wheat in the grain store. I'll put rat poison in my barrels of cider and down the well, then I'll grab my old lady and my shotgun and run like hell.'

Our village hall had been requisitioned by the military, serving as a billet for soldiers, many of whom had endured the trauma of Dunkirk. The venue for the proposed meeting was therefore the parish schoolroom, a matter of necessity rather than choice.

There was much shuffling, grunting and complaining as full-grown men and well-upholstered ladies tried to fold their limbs and excess weight into child-sized seats and desks.

A large map of our village, divided into different coloured sections, was pinned to the blackboard. A gloomy, doom-laden Civil Defence 'advisor', who looked as if he did undertaking and embalming as a day job, warned us of the increasing possibility of heavy bombing raids, and that while no one could stand and argue with high explosive bombs, incendiary fires could well be contained if patrolling couples were trained and equipped to deal with them quickly.

Our speaker explained that he now required twelve volunteers of either sex from each coloured section, still uninvolved with The Special Constabulary, First Aid, The Auxiliary Fire Service, for the new force to be known as the Local Defence Volunteers.

Enough hands had been raised to reach the required quota for each section, but finding twelve people happily volunteering to spend long hours patrolling with their neighbours was a totally different proposition. There was considerable hubbub and discussion. No one cared to stand up and publicly voice the honest objection that they did not relish spending night after night on fire watch with a neighbour whose existence they had refused to acknowledge for years.

The Dwyers and the Woodsteps were a case in point. Living in adjoining houses, they shared a communal garden path to their back-to-back privies, and yet their complex family feud was of such long standing that they paid no more attention to each other than they would have given to a passing ant.

It would have taken more than a fire bomb to get the relatives of Wilf Woodstep and Diddler Dwyer stirrup pumping together. Solomon himself would have been hard put to decide the truthfulness of the allegation that Diddler had done the shameful deed of tempting Daisy Woodstep in the woodshed, heaping dishonour on dishonour by blaming Daisy's 'lump' on the coalman who had been seen delivering a couple of extra sacks of 'nutty slack'.

No midnight patrolling could offer a convincing explanation for the fact that when all the rest of the numerous Dwyer offspring were brown-eyed and dark-haired, one little lad looked exactly like other little Woodsteps, Wilf in miniature, including his blue eyes, hooked nose and flaming red hair. This was neither the time nor the place to air such a delicate topic to a high and mighty stranger, too unversed in country ways to understand.

There was something of a hiatus, with much mumbling and shuffling of feet until Charlie Flambit spoke up. Blushing scarlet, Charlie said that while he was willing to defend his own patch and indeed that of his neighbour, bitter personal experience had taught him that eight hours of the night spent in the company of certain maiden lady sisters could well result in a simple chap like him getting snotty letters from solicitors, with the threat of being sued in court.

'Come now! My good man! Don't you know there's a war on? I see no great sacrifice or danger in doing one's share of fire watching with a neighbour, male or female.'

Stung to a rare flush of anger, Charlie retorted somewhat heatedly, 'I don't suppose you do, mister, but then those two pestering old biddies down the lane ain't been trying to get their hooks into you for the last twenty years. It wasn't you who got coerced into doing a neighbourly turn when they pleaded for help to get a trapped bird out of their bedroom chimney, just when a chap was going home from work come Saturday dinner time. You were not expected to traipse bootless round the place for fear of marking their carpets, or clear up all the soot and mess it made getting the old jackdaw down. Let me tell you, mister, that listening to them scheming females fair made me wonder if they intended to keep me shut up with them as a household pet. I was so anxious to get away I slipped off home by taking a short cut over the back garden hedge, clean forgetting that I'd left my working jacket and bait basket hanging on their front gatepost, with my barrow and dung fork just inside their front garden, until I was getting set to go to work that following Monday.

'You haven't had Arethusa and Miriam Pringe constantly complaining that you had a bounden duty to wed one or the other of them because they reckoned you had besmirched their unsullied names, hateful gossip implying that it was not only your bait basket, working jacket and weskit that had stayed with them all weekend. When a chap gets an official letter claiming that he's caused them Pringe females grievous stress and ruined their reputations by taking a jackdaw out of their chimney, just imagine the misery a night out under the stars with either of them would cause. I've dodged them too long to risk it! We'll have to have a different strike out than your fancy plan.'

At this point Miss Miriam Pringe enlivened the proceedings by turning to point her umbrella in Charlie's direction, while declaiming: 'You clodhopping Casanova!' before fluttering to the floor in a dramatic swoon.

The Civil Defence speaker called the meeting to order, saying that he could waste no more time on fatuous rural feuds and inanities. We must sort out the matter of rosters for ourselves.

I was issued with a tin hat and 'One Whistle – Civil Defence Personnel For The Use Of', half-shares in a long-handled shovel and a stirrup pump, all signed for on a form of acknowledgement in which I promised to hand them back to the government after hostilities ceased. A warrant card authorized me free access to any conflagration caused by enemy action.

Our section of the village had the least difficulty in arranging our fire-watching roster. In fact we came to an amicable but highly irregular arrangement. This ignored the stupidity of two fire watchers mooching around in the dark one night in six, when one person could keep watch on their own quite adequately. According to our scheme, by taking turns we could all have eleven nights' sound sleep without a break – God and the Luftwaffe willing.

Almost without exception, we were all working long hours in various food-producing occupations and, as old Harry Apple-thorn said, 'Jerry didn't send his bombers over wearing soft-soled carpet slippers.' As soon as the anti-aircraft guns opened up, and the bombers came over, we were all awake and ready to deal with the situation, and the sound of the watcher on duty blasting forth on a whistle travelled far in the quiet country night air.

On watch towards dawn one moonless night, with no distant siren wailing a warning, I heard a low-flying plane come in over the coastal marshes and pass overhead before turning out towards the sea again. I imagined that an eerie sighing sound in the sky above me came from a flock of night-flying lapwing and gave the matter no thought until the following day when our village policeman asked if I had heard anything strange during my spell on fire watch.

As I told him about the low-flying aircraft and the weird noises after it had passed over, he explained that someone had heard re-peated whistle blasts coming from the two-miles-distant creek, then hidden by a low-lying mist. At break of day he had cycled over that way to investigate and met old Bill Boorchase, red-faced, still blasting forth on a whistle as he hurried along the lane, his braces dangling, holding up his breeches as he ran. Greeting the policeman like a long-lost brother, he voiced his complaint.

'What would old Hitler want to pick on me for? It won't help him to win the war by putting me off my regular morning routine. I'm not one to make a fuss, but a chap can't sit comfort-able on the throne, smoking his pipe and contemplating the wonders of nature, with a dirty great parachute mine dangling in the bowed-down branches of his apple tree above his privy roof.'

Unwilling to go to heaven with his breeches round his ankles, Bill had run in panic. The policeman's suggestion that he found a quiet place behind a hedge, and a couple of dock leaves, re-ceived the derision it deserved. By way of afterthought, our guardian of the law warned that all windows and doors must be left open. A Royal Navy bomb squad was dismantling the huge mine that could have left roofless houses for miles.

When the mine was eventually defused and taken to the deso-late estuary saltings for a controlled explosion, the shock wave sent plates flying off the shelf of the kitchen dresser, but our little country corner felt able to breathe again.

The problem of collecting the stirrup pump and shovel from the various fire watchers on our list was simply solved by dumping them in the hollow ash tree near the lanes crossroads before the next one went on duty. The co-ordinator of local air-raid precautions insisted on occasional fire-fighting practices. As I learned the intricacies of stirrup pump maintenance, I realized the possibilities this heaven-sent appliance offered. With a bit of initiative, this could be the quick answer to giving the cowshed walls and Mum's chicken houses a much-needed coat of lime-wash.

I mixed the whitewash by the bucketful, my mother straining it through three layers of butter muslin to make sure it did not clog up the works. We tackled this highly irregular activity on the afternoon and evening before I was due to go on fire watch. I sprayed the cowshed by lantern light, with all doors shut in compliance with the blackout regulations. The pump had worked beyond all expectations and the job was done before ten.

I was washing whitewash off the stirrup pump when the sound of distant gunfire and approaching heavy-engined aircraft preceded the air-raid sirens sounding in the distant town.

The anti-aircraft battery on the marsh edge went into action. I ran to fetch my whistle, shovel, and tin hat. A considerable amount of shrapnel was whistling down and an enemy aircraft, caught in the glare of searchlights, jettisoned its bomb load out across the marshes.

Standing under the crossroads ash tree until the sound of gunfire and aircraft engines faded, I saw the glow-worm light of a blackout regulation masked cycle lamp and the dark outline of the rider approaching along the lane. The unknown cyclist seemed to brake sharply, to the accompanying sound of skidding tyres on gravel. There was no time to ascertain the cause of this sudden change of direction because the red reflection of the cycle rear light was disappearing back down the lane at considerable speed.

Somewhat mystified, I went home to clean the whitewash spatters off my face and change into something more suitable for fire watching than my cowshed decorating old white cotton overall.

Before my next stint of fire watching, our somewhat anxious postman, Perce, approached my father, expressing his doubts about the wisdom of using the old hollow ash tree as the collecting point for our stirrup pump.

He confided the cause of his apprehension: 'Heaven alone knows I'm not one given over to having fanciful notions and I'd probably get drummed out of the Special Constabulary if I told anyone else, but the other night I was out on patrol when I saw a figure all in white and still as a statue, standing under the old ash tree. I tell you, Harry, I broke out in a cold muck sweat. A sight like that could leave a young maid like your Jo half frit to death.'

'Most likely,' Dad answered drily.

Thereafter Post Hole Willy's garden shed became the nerve centre of our fire watching group's activities, our stirrup pump being afforded pride of place on a nail behind the door. Officially our main weapon of defence, this was never actually used in anger, except for repelling the invasion of greenfly on Perce's roses, and blackfly on Willy's broad beans.

When the Luftwaffe scattered their litter around indiscriminately, we found that the quickest and most effective method of extinguishing incendiary bombs was by shovelling dirt on them, or even a wet cowpat that providence had dropped close at hand.

In a vulnerable area with the possibility of invasion still very real, everyone was warned to report any unusual activities. One night when a full bright 'bombers' moon transformed the scenery into a symphony of shadowy blue and silver, my fire-watching patrol was made hideous by the incessant bellowing of our love-sick shorthorn cow. Dolly had reared seven calves in her time and was old enough to know better than to work herself into a frenzy.

Out across the moonlit fields came the answering love call of Sir Jasper, Charlie Cartwright's Hereford bull. They kept up their love duet for a couple of hours, then all was silence except for the rustlings and snufflings of a countryside asleep on a warm summer-scented night.

The crop of tall-stemmed beans in Starve Crow Field were all in bloom, the night air heavy with the fragrant scent that was believed in early centuries to drive men mad. As I cycled past idly wondering if this was what had driven Dolly and Sir Jasper mad with desire, I heard rustling amongst the bean rows for several directions.

Standing on my bike pedals I saw definite movement. Several creatures, human or otherwise, were creeping across the field. If they were Nazi parachutists, I was not going to hang around to fight them with my shovel. I rushed back home, tore upstairs and woke my hard working, sleep-deprived Dad.

Half awake, having lain listening to our bellowing Dolly hour after hour, he was less than ecstatic to be told that there were probably dozens of parachutists trampling around in our bean field. Perhaps they had even slaughtered Dolly to keep her quiet.

'Or maybe she's broke out and is up in Starve Crow with the others, bloating themselves fit to burst,' Dad grumbled.

With horses in the stable and all the other terrified farm live-stock to fend for during air raids, he too had lacked the luxury of restful sleep. He told me to get the rook gun down from the beam rack, and a box of cartridges, just in case we were taking on the Third Reich.

We hurried to the pasture to find it empty. Dolly had broken down the fence and gone courting, taking Gert and Daisy, two other elderly milking cows with her, along with a couple of dozen calves, young heifers and steers.

Trying to track cattle through a dew-soaked, tall-stalked bean field by moonlight was extremely unrewarding, especially when my father suddenly raised his gun and shouted, 'Got you, you bugger! Put your hands up!'

A soldier with a black face and with several bean stalks camouflaging his tin helmet slowly rose, muttering in broadest cockney, 'Strewf, mate, you didn't 'arf put the wind up me. Bloody 'ell!'

With the army out on a night exercise it was no use looking for our stray cattle until daylight. We gave up in disgust and went home.

I found our bovine absconders soon after daybreak. They were in one of Charlie Cartwright's meadows, circling round a weary-looking Hereford bull. Sir Jasper tottered slowly to his hooves at my approach, looking as if all he asked of life at that moment was to be left in peace.

Dolly was the boss cow of our cattle and, like Gert and Daisy, was well aware that it was past the time when she was usually milked. Reminding her that I wanted no skittish behaviour, but expected her to lead the rest home along the lanes instead of the cross-country route she had taken overnight, I grabbed her tail and began the long walk back.

Plodding along with the other escapees ambling homeward behind us, we passed the village hall. Called to attention by their sergeant, a crowd of soldiers lining up for their breakfast cheered us on our way home.

The Farmer Wants a Wife

A torrential, sleety downpour sent Jordan Barbond hurrying to take shelter beneath the flapping canvas awning of the self-styled 'Dr Barker's Farm Remedies and Theraputic Medicines' stall. As sheets of scudding rain and hail drove across the cobbles of the almost-deserted cattle market, he was joined by an elderly drover whose lifelong aversion to soap, razors, or clean clothing lead most people to believe he had been named 'Whiffy' rather than Wilfred Spurge from birth. Two ever-watchful rough-coated crossbred collie dogs slunk down by Whiffy's feet, growling a menacing duet of warning as Jordan attempted to move upwind of the malodorous drover. Scarcely tolerable at the best of times, the smell of unkempt dogs and their owner was intensified prodigiously when they were wet. With two pairs of wary canine eyes observing his every movement, Jordan stayed where he was, intuition rapidly becoming absolute conviction that he would have fared much better if he had stayed at home.

Whiffy ruminated on his quid of chewing tobacco as he gazed across at the few pens of rain-soaked barren cows, scrawny old ewes, and pathetic baby veal calves, observing that the market day following after Christmas was usually about as lively as the elastic in Big Maggie's Sunday garters. He could personally vouch that on both counts, this year was the slackest of them all.

Jordan agreed that no livestock awaiting auction was worth waiting around to bid for in the wet. As soon as the rain eased, he intended to nip smartly across Market Street to the tobacconists for his weekly ounce of 'Nosegay' and half-pound of peppermint lumps, then head homewards. He asked the old market drover when he thought the rain would stop.

Whiffy's locally acknowledged reputation as a weather prophet had been earned the hard way, his observance of the changing patterns of the seasons gleaned from boyhood days when he slept under haystacks, hedges, or barn roofs, travelling the green droving roads with a father who took cattle herds, sheep, and even flocks of geese across the depth and breadth of the three countries, walking all the way.

Whiffy regretted that those days and country ways had virtually vanished. He still preferred to roam abroad rather than to sleep beneath the sagging thatch of the shanty he called home.

Oblivious of the rain streaming off the edge of the awning, Whiffy glanced out at the sky, shrugged his shoulders, and shook his head as he voiced his opinion of the weather prospects.

'If you'm hoping to wait and stay dry, you'll be stood standing yere tomorrow. Why do them as make such a mortal hullaballoo about barbering, bathing, washing every day, and clean drawers every Sunday, allus get in such a pother when they are caught out in a bit of natural-falling rain? If you be likely to melt like salt or sugar in the wet, Jordan lad, I ain't. I reckon I've timed it just right to go over by the selling ring and stand close by Moses Mason and his brandy flask. If I takes my tin cup out ready, he'll be gentleman enough to pour a quick nip to help me on my way.'

Pausing only to cock their legs against the stall trestle stays, Whiffy's dogs cast one last malevolent growling glance in Jordan's direction and followed their master out into the rain.

Watching the drover's departure with some satisfaction, the

top-hatted, frock-coated owner of the stall uncorked a bottle of strong-smelling rubbing oils, spattering it around in the manner of an old-time priest offering benediction. The pungent aromatic vapours set Jordan's eyes watering as the horse doctor heaved a heartfelt sigh of relief.

'Phew! Whiffy might be nearing eighty, but he doesn't improve with keeping. He drives customers away faster than a swarm of hornets. The auctioneer's clerk was all for dunking him and a bottle of Jeyes Fluid in the horse tough at the back end of summer, but it was agreed that no beast would be persuaded to drink from it afterwards. Has he no relatives to take him in hand, Jordan? Not that I would relish the prospect. Can you imagine sharing a roof with him and his flea-bag dogs? Imagine having to call him Dad.'

Agreeing that the prospect did not bear contemplation, Jordan turned up his raincoat collar and hurried on his way.

The tobacconist and sweet shop in Market Street had remained virtually unaltered for the century or more that it had been owned and run by three generations of the same family. It had a small-paned front window, three interior walls lined with dark varnished cupboards and drawered cabinets, and a polished counter cluttered with small glass dishes of pipe or cigarette tobacco, hand-printed labels adorning 'Nut Brown', 'Nosegay', 'Rough Cut', and the like. Jars of sweets lined the shelves on the front window wall, effectively blocking off most of the natural light. The gaslight above the counter hissed and spluttered. A brass cowbell danced on a spring as Jordan entered the latched door.

A brown-dressed, brown-haired, brown-eyed woman emerged from behind a brown plush curtain. Jordan, who had been a regular customer ever since he was man enough to help his father load pigs for market, had always regarded Miss Iris as a pleasant, unchanging fixture of the shop. Her older brother, Alfred, followed behind her, intent on an unhurried chat. It was that kind of shop. They asked if Jordan had enjoyed a happy Christmas.

'Wonderful!' he responded sardonically. 'Absolutely marvellous! Some holly-pinching idiot unchained the bottom paddock gate on the afternoon of Christmas Eve, so the stiff-legged old mare I turned out for a few hours' exercise each day wandered out into a field of kale, along with some thirty bullocks. Consequently my Christmas Day was spent unsuccessfully trying to save her from a severe attack of colic. The elderly lady who cooks and cleans for me twice a week put a bit of dinner on the stove for me early on Christmas morning, but by the time I could get back to eat it, there was only charcoaled potatoes, cremated chicken, a pudding boiled dry, and a ruined saucepan.'

Intent on weighing out mint lumps, Miss Iris suggested that farming must be a lonely way to earn a living, without a wife.

'There aren't many of them about!' Jordan told her. 'When you live down the end of a lonely lane, prospective brides are a bit thin on the ground. You can't go to markets, fairs or sales to study what likely lassies there are on offer in the same way you could bid for a good working horse.'

Brother and sister discussed Jordan's dilemma objectively, agreeing that farming eighty remote acres offered little opportunity for courtship, with time no longer on his side. Miss Iris suggested it might pay to advertise. The three-pence-a-week postcards on the board in the shop window were very successful. Blushing scarlet, Jordan said that even if he knew what to write, a postcard would never work.

Alfred, scribbling, asked 'What about "Farmer seeks honest country-loving companion. Matrimony in mind."' The arrival of another customer hastily settled the matter. Jordan paid a shilling for four weeks' advertizing, and wished all present a Happy New Year.

The possible implications of this venture assumed nightmare proportions once he was back home. He had lived alone since the death of his mother fifteen years previously. Did he really want some bossy female ploughing through his placid life? A fortnight passed before he had enough courage to buy his usual mint lumps and pipe tobacco.

His fears were groundless. No one had replied.

On the fourth week his resolve to end such nonsense was shattered. In a note left by a well-dressed, well-spoken lady was the simple message: 'Corner seat. Corner café. Market Day. 2 p.m. sharp.'

Attempting to quell Jordan's rising panic, Alfred reminded him that he could always walk out if he did not like the look of the lady in the café corner seat. Miss Iris suggested that he concentrate his mind on a lifetime of cooked dinners, hot breakfasts and slippers warming by the fire as he set off for his two o'clock date.

As soon as Jordan tentatively entered the tea room, a tweedy, well-built woman half rose and waved from the corner seat. He felt like a rabbit being driven into a poacher's net. Miss Betty had ordered tea and cakes, and was obviously determined to approach their meeting in a workmanlike manner. She said that at forty, she was too mature to play the coy maiden, preferring to discuss the matter in hand without any foolish romantic nonsense. She would be available to keep house on a permanent basis within a month, and providing both were agreeable, marry him as soon as arrangements could be made after that.

When Jordan next called at the shop, he was happy to tell Miss Iris and Alfred that his new friend Betty could well be a great help and comfort. On her first afternoon visit, his cluttered kitchen had undergone a complete transformation. She was obviously not afraid of hard work.

A few days later, Jordan spent from daybreak to dark away from home attending a ram sale. He returned to find Betty in residence. She had spent the day rearranging the house from top to bottom, dumping anything she regarded as 'old rubbish' on a huge bonfire, including his farming records and financial accounts. She had cooked an evening meal, over which she spoke of the changes she intended to make.

The final straw that made Jordan decide he must break free from her was the pinch of snuff she took before lighting an after-dinner cigar. She suggested that since she was there to stay, they might as well begin as they meant to go on and keep each other warm at night. Jordan hastily retired, bolting his bedroom door.

Early the next morning, Jordan went into town intent on seeking help and advice from Miss Iris and Alfred, holding them partially responsible for his plight. He happened to encounter old Whiffy and his dogs, looking more disreputable than ever. A remark made by the horse doctor on that post-Christmas market day, surfaced in his mind.

Welcoming Whiffy like a much-loved friend, Jordan asked how he would like to be given ten pounds, a good hot meal, and a warm bed for the night. The matter was urgent. He would explain the situation on the way.

Jordan's predicament with his snuff-sniffing, cigar-smoking, forceful fiancée appealed to Whiffy's sense of humour. He promised that he would help resolve matters by having a good scratch.

Alighting from Jordan's pick-up truck, complete with the two dogs, they trailed through the muddy yard and across the freshly scrubbed kitchen floor. Jordan called ever-busy Betty from the pantry.

'Betty! Wonderful news. My Dad has given up roaming and decided to come home to live now you are here to look after us.'

Forgetting she was a lady, Betty swore roundly, saying she would not stay under the same roof as a stinking old tramp and his mangy, flea-bag dogs. Leering gummily, Whiffy told her that she would have to if she intended to remain, since the place belonged to him. His son Jordan owned nothing at all.

Chuckling as the lady departed in high dudgeon, Whiffy remarked that in pretending to be related to Jordan, he had come closer to the mark than his farming friend could guess. He could well have been an uncle, Jordan's aunt having been one of the local lassies Whiffy had chased after and sometimes caught, back in the days when he was young and foolish enough to take the occasional bath.

On the next visit to the tobacconist's, Jordan sheepishly acquainted Miss Iris and her brother with the farcical situation, expressing his thanks that the card in the window had not inspired more offers.

Miss Iris looked up from weighing out his tobacco, speaking softly: 'Did it never occur to you that postcards were unnecessary? In all these years, did you never see me as anything but the woman behind the counter?'

Jordan was surprised to hear himself admit that he thought of her as someone unattainable. Miss Iris unlatched the counter flap and pulled aside the brown plush curtain, offering the invitation: 'Come through and I will make us all a nice cup of tea.'

Uncle Noah's Ark

Disconsolate on the hearth-stoned doorstep, Alec stood munching his bread and dripping in the early morning sunshine as he watched two groups of Sunday School scholars, mustering at each side of the village green as if they were opposing armies. Two lumbering motor coaches from rival companies approached each other like jousting knights, stopping to parley, cab to cab, establishing which group was 'Chapel' and which was 'Church'.

Food hampers, tall white enamelled jugs of lemonade with butter muslin tied round the top to keep flies out, ubiquitous lidded slop pails and latecomers were bundled aboard. With each outing party determined to get away first, they set off in an intensity of cheering and singing, departing on receding sound waves, bound for the same seaside beaches for their annual Summer Treat.

Silence settled around Alec as if some giant sweeping brush had cleared the village green. All itchy, spotty, red-eyed with misery and measles, he seemed momentarily to be the only speck of humanity left on the scene. The silence was soon shattered.

'Alec! Don't stand out there moping and mooning. Time's a-wasting. You know I want to get an early start.'

His mother's sharp-spoken voice established the fact that being 'measles-banished' from the Sunday School outing did not preclude him for helping her earn a few extra shillings fruit picking while they had the chance.

The number of pickers absent on the outing trips this Saturday morning meant that a special bonus rate was being offered to anyone helping to gather enough green gooseberries to fulfil the fruit farm's contracted quota to a jam factory in the nearest town.

At eleven years old and growing fast, Alec was deemed capable of contributing toward providing winter clothing, since his legs were getting longer than those of his trousers, and his jacket sleeves kept parting company with his wrists. The fact that he was still highly infectious was overlooked, his mother having been told that he could pick downwind of any other helpers with infants in pushchairs.

Apart from a few gipsy children, all the rest were on their day trips except Alec, and if he shed a few measles germs among the gooseberries he picked, what harm could come of it when they were to be boiled up in the giant vats of jam?

The morning sun climbed to its zenith, gaining strength, relentlessly beating down on the parched, dusty gooseberry field. Beset with nettles and sharp-spined thistles, the rows of green bushes seemed to stretch out to infinity, as Alec thought longingly of rock pools, ice cream cones, and cool tide-wet sand, soft between his toes. His mother, perching on a low stool, glared through the spiky gooseberry bush, calling to him to stop daydreaming and pick.

Alec's Uncle Pete, the fruit farm carter, led his horse and waggon up between the lines of bushes to collect the two bushel boxes they had filled. He joked about all the sweets Alec would be able to buy with the picking money he had earned.

'With all your Sunday School outing spending money and a sub on today's earnings, I expect you'll be down at the shop buying sherbert dabs and liquorice toffee come bait time.'

'He's not going anywhere while he's still contagious, so stop filling his head with rubbish!' Alec's Mum responded, sour-faced as if she had been eating the gooseberries they were picking. Always ready to haggle with her husband's happy-go-lucky bachelor brother, she sniffed disparagingly. 'No wonder you have never saved or settled if you practise what you preach to others. I'll thank you not to encourage your brother's son in such extravagant spendthrift ways. Why would he be given spending money when he wasn't going to the outing to need it? It costs enough to keep him looking decent and tidy as it is.'

'Poor little dab looks as if he could do with a bit of cheer and comfort, missus, and you can tell brother Phil I said so. By the way, just remind him we promised to go down to old Uncle Noah Striggs come Lammastide weekend, to shift his ark. Perhaps the boy could come with us to lend a hand if you will let him, Katey. Come on, girl, loosen up a bit and smile.'

'Not so much of the Katey!' Alec watched his mother's face grow crimson and soften, her eyes smiling for an instant. 'If Alec looks as peeky as you make out, he might not be strong enough to go with you by the first weekend in August. We'll have to wait and see.'

The cart moved away, mother and son continued to pick gooseberries, Alec now trying to please. 'Wait and see' was as far as his Mum ever went to agreeing at the first attempt at asking. He knew better than to pursue the subject of going off with his father and uncle, when the mere mention of their relatives always brought a thin-lipped scowl of disapproval to his mother's face. Even as they were picking, she was obviously pondering the prospect of his going on this duty mission.

'I'll not have you learning rough ways from them old heathens. Heaven knows it took me long enough to get your father trained into respectable civilized ways.'

'Yes, Mum, no, Mum,' Alec answered at appropriate pauses in her cryptic observations.

'I'll not forget the first time your father took me over to introduce me to them. I'd worn my best velour hat and put it on the dresser shelf because there was nowhere to hang it. It was completely ruined. One of the cackling bantams the old man allowed to trail in and out as if the kitchen was a fowl pen, had laid an egg in the crown and messed all over the brim.'

Alec hid his smile behind a tall dock plant. The hot wearying hours wore on.

As his Uncle Pete came to collect the last fruit boxes of the day, he offered Alec something wriggling, wrapped round in a red spotted handkerchief, telling him to handle it gently.

'Today has been no Sunday School treat for you, has it, nipper? I found this on the road and wondered if you could try and keep it alive until I can get it over to Uncle Noah.'

'Now what rubbish are you lumbering him with?' His mother sounded hot, tired and cross. Alec uncovered a frightened baby bird.

Assuring him that the indeterminate feathered fledgling was a young magpie that had probably been injured falling from a nest, his Uncle Pete gave him a quick conspiratorial wink. Alec knew that magpies could be trained to mimic all sorts of sounds. He tucked it inside his shirt, hoping it was not susceptible to measles. It stayed there giving an occasional cheep and flutter until it was time to go home.

Alec's father lined an apple crate with hay and sheep's wool, showing him how to stuff chopped worms, bread scraps, and bits of suet into the noisy squawking beak that, within hours of bringing the bird home, came open like a lid every time he went near.

'Terribly unlucky things to have in the house, magpies,' his father muttered just within his mother's hearing. 'We don't want to keep it here messing the place up and annoying your mother unnecessarily, so I'll be glad to pass it over to your Great-Uncle Noah. He had a one-legged goose, a three-legged goat, and fox cub that thought it was a kitten, last time we went over. You would have to come on the back of my bike to get it there.'

Alec's mother glared accusingly at the pair of them from the far side of the kitchen table.

'That wretched bird is part of a plot to make me let Alec go gallivanting off with you and Pete, isn't it? Never mind that your crazy-headed old aunt and uncle act uncouth and live rough as pigs in a sty. You want to take him to get his clothes messed up and probably come home filthy dirty, do you?'

Momentarily Alec saw all hopes of a Lammastide break fading like mist in sunlight, but then he heard his father responding decisively, with a rare authoritarian tone to his voice.

'That's right, Kate! We are taking the lad with us. There's no

cause for you to worry or create a fuss. Pit digging and ark moving
are not what anyone would call gallivanting. Alec's not going on
an outing you would call a treat, so there's no argument to be
made. Let's hope the fine weather holds for the weekend after
next.'

Alec had heard anecdotes about the eccentricities of his
Great-Uncle Noah and Great-Aunt Araminta for as long as he
could remember, not to mention his mother's scorn for people
who could let their chicken lay eggs in their nephew's nicely
brought-up fiancée's hat. It was almost worth catching the measles to be going on this jaunt to stay with them. Almost, but not
quite.

By Lammastide the rash had faded and the baby magpie had
become a demanding, strutting, raucous young bird, transported
in a cloth-covered shopping basket held by Alec as he rode on
the back carrier of his father's bike.

His Dad and Uncle Pete had ridden sedately through the village, but as they pedalled the long miles across country, they
whistled and sang as if they were a couple of carefree boys let out
of school. To Alec the journey was one glorious adventure. They
stopped at a wayside public house, where Alec was allowed to sit
in a cool corner drinking ginger beer from a stone bottle with a
marble stopper, the jolly lady behind the bar laughing and joking
with Uncle Pete and Alec's father, calling them her 'lovely lads'.

Turning down a dead-end track, they came to the gateway of
an old house that wore a thatched roof much as if it was a warm
hat to be pulled down over its ears. Great-Uncle Noah stood
leaning on a five-barred gate, looking much like his namesake in
Alec's Sunday School scripture book, all smocked, white-
bearded, his shoulder-length silver hair round his head. He
greeted Alec with an unrestrained hug.

'So you're going to help me move my ark closer to the top end
of the garden? By the time it actually gets close to the hedge, I
doubt if Minty and me will be around to need it any more. We
worked it out see, thinking we might have sixty years together
from the day we were wed, if we were lucky.

'I measured out a sixtieth of the garden and dug the first pit,
then built the prettiest privy a bride could wish for to put over it.
I've kept it in good order, never failing to move it forward a sixtieth each Lammastide regular. Come you, boy, and look.'

Alec expressed his admiration for the ornate edifice resembling a larger version of a double sedan chair, complete with handles at the side, much like those one used to convey gentry through muddy streets.

Cats, dogs, chickens, a pig called George and the three-legged goat wandered into the house at will. The wrinkles on Great-Aunt Minty's grimy face resembled lines on a sea chart marking some narrow tidal channel. Each quavering corncrake word she uttered brought her pointed chin into closer proximity to her nose, but her eyes were shiny bright and dark as ivy berries. They smiled whenever she spoke. She doled out a massive meal of mutton stew, followed by treacle pudding and custard, all washed down with home-made nettle beer.

'I'd surmise that this yere boy needs building up a bit before he goes pit digging,' Great-Aunt Minty announced after they had eaten. 'I've got a little job for him. Them perishing greenfly are sucking the life out of my moss rose bushes, and not a ladybird in sight. Go you then, boy, and fetch I back a pail of wet weed. There's no finer way to stop them. You'll find cartloads of the stuff laying around if you go to the end of the lane.'

Having been raised by his mother to believe that children must never question or argue with their elders, Alec was puzzled by his great-aunt's instructions, wondering if he would recognize wet weed if he saw any, wherever the cartloads of them might grow.

His Uncle Pete found him an old pail to hang on the handlebars as he wheeled out his father's high-saddled bike, and told him there was no need to hurry back until he felt hungry. Maybe his Mum had been right in her assumption that old Noah and Araminta were potty. By her standards they were certainly less than fastidious. She had dusted his socks and pyjamas with Keatings Flea Powder before he left home, convinced that he might catch lice.

And yet there was an unbelievable feeling of happiness about this place, a total lack of tension. No one here would have a mood because his bootlaces were undone.

Alec found himself singing as he rode along the high-banked lane lined with scabious, dog rose and honeysuckle until the track disappeared amid high dunes of sand. Beyond lay a wide expanse of sunlit ocean, blue as the sky, a world away from the

overcrowded pebble beaches of remembered Sunday School out-
ings. Now he could stand in awe and wonder, sharing the shore
with no one but a few gulls noisily scavenging among the wet
seaweed fringing the tideline on the sand. This then was what he
had been sent to gather by smiling elders who had told him there
was no need to hurry back.

He ran to the edge of the sea, his studded country boots im-
printing the smooth clean sand. Within seconds they were off his
feet and round his neck. Raised by a mother who considered that
cold water washes prevented boys from becoming 'cissies', Alec
found the sun-warmed sea pleasant to his bare toes. A wavelet
lapped periously close to his trousers legs. Knowing that getting
his best flannels dirty would earn him a hiding from his mother,
he retreated from the water to shed his clothes, leaving them
above the high-water mark.

Strictly a nonswimmer, since he had never had the chance to
learn, he raced back into the shallows, splashing and floundering
around as happily as a young duckling in a drinking trough. He
lay at full length in the knee-deep water, relaxed and contented,
discovering that he had mastered the art of floating. This fantas-
tic weightless sensation was wonderful until a wave washed over
his face.

Instinctively he put down his feet to stand up, but his toes had
great difficulty in touching the bottom. In a moment of panic he
realized he had drifted out; the water was now up to his chest.
Putting his arms forward because his feet would not stay down,
he wriggled first one leg, then the other forward. By marvellous
accident he found that he was propelling himself towards the
shore, his 'dog paddle' stroke enabling him to swim.

Confident now that nothing was impossible in this magical
place, he wandered along the beach, finding a lukewarm rock
pool to lie in, luxuriating in the sun. He had no way of knowing
how long he stayed there, except that the tide was coming in and
the sun had moved to a different part of the sky. Hearing shouts
of laughter coming from the direction of the dunes, he saw his
father and uncle riding, one on the saddle, one on the pedals of
his uncle's bike before tumbling in a heap on the sand.

They waved as he called to them from a distance. Astounded,
he watched them shedding their clothes, stripping stark naked,
plunging into the waves, swimming as easily as eels. The sharp

contrast between their sun-browned arms, necks and faces, and their white bodies, made them look like russet apples three-quarters peeled.

Alec's own legs resembled wrinkled sticks of macaroni. He moved up the beach to dry off in the afternoon sun. It seemed as if his father's swim had washed away the lines on his face, making him look years younger.

'We could do a spot of night fishing,' his uncle suggested as they all rode back along the track. Uncle Noah's ornate ark was now safely installed in a new position. Alec was warned not to linger bare-bottomed on the seat longer than necessary because the lime in the pit was liable to give off heat. He had no intention of lingering anywhere. There was bait to dig, feather lures to untangle, fishing line to check.

Expecting that just his father, his uncle, and himself would be going night fishing, he was surprised to see that the old couple were going with them, followed by a blind dog, a goat called Emily and a cat.

His father and uncle hauled an old hand cart down the track, while he walked beside the biblical-looking old man and the little old lady who scuttled along like a mouse. She had found an odd selection of garments for him to wear on the beach so that his good clothes would not get spoiled.

The masthead lights of two fishing boats danced a duet in a silver path of moonlight across the water. Alec thought himself to be the luckiest lad in the world. They lit a driftwood fire to cook the fish that only Great-Uncle Noah seemed able to catch. Great-Aunt Minty lit a lantern, setting it down on an old table-cloth. The lamplight shone on a basin of butter, three cottage loaves, and a stone jar of elderflower wine.

Dawn was creeping over the eastern horizon before Alec settled down under an eiderdown on the straw mattress he shared with his father, but he was wide awake again before seven o'clock. On that Sunday morning, he helped his uncle and father saw a huge heap of log wood, then went with them back to the shore for a final swim. By mid-afternoon, Alec was as tidily dressed as his Mum would have wished, his father's face growing ever more sombre as they rode the long miles home.

'No need to tell you mother we kept you up all night, and that you spent most of yesterday up to your neck in water. She wouldn't be keen to know about me swimming either. Uncle Noah's world isn't hers. She would want no part of it. There are things women don't understand and us men wouldn't want them to know.'

Alec's mother called out in greeting from the doorway.

'I've got the copper water hot and the tin bath ready for the pair of you. I don't suppose your skin has had a wash since you left here. I hope Alec's not picked up anything nasty from those old heathens.'

'No, Kate,' her husband reassured her. 'We've just done the usual, digging a pit and moving Uncle's ark.' A quick secret smile passed between father and son, as he added: 'Don't worry. I made sure Alec had a wash.'

An Elemental Force

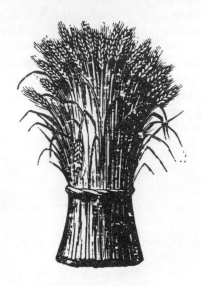

On that October morning, Rest Harrow Field and the wooded hills beyond seemed so timeless and remote from the hostilities of belligerent mankind, I understood why old villagers still gave credence to old superstitions, believing that the whim of some strange elemental force governed the weather and dictated the fertility of livestock and the soil. Straw plaited corn maidens or dollies still graced many farmstead kitchens and barns. Elusive earth spirits must be placated and encouraged to linger by time-honoured ritual in quiet communion with the land.

Free as the wheeling gulls and crested lapwings circling around me, I drove our old cleated iron-wheeled Fordson tractor back and forth, trying to plough a straight furrow across the twenty-acre field. Faded yellow leaves, once the brave green medals of summer, danced on a west wind, setting the swirling smoke from

Dad's hedge-cuttings bonfire in the next field racing up over the hill as if it had a will of its own.

I was pitchforked out of the realms of whimsy with a jolt, suddenly aware of the cold realities of wartime farming as the plough jerked, making loud metallic clunking noises, piling soil high around the vertical cutting coulter as the tractor engine coughed in protest and died.

Almost instinctively I switched off the fuel line and ran. Much unwanted metal had littered down from our country skies during the preceding war years. During the previous spring I had repeatedly driven over what I had imagined to be a partially buried piece of scrap water pipe among the stones filling the potholes on the edge of the farm track, until a harrow tine inadvertently hauled it to the surface and we realized that is was a small unexploded bomb. A couple of cheerfully whistling soldiers carried it away in a sand-filled latrine bucket, taking it down to the saltings beyond the marsh sea wall to detonate it. For a small bomb it made a surprisingly loud report.

Then, of course, there was the neat, yard-wide hole that Charlie Cartwright almost fell into while cutting cattle feed in his kale field. This evoked far wider interest. The shining boots of many military and civilian bigwigs were soiled by tracking through Charlie's bullock yards, ankle-deep in muck. The bomb disposal team who set up camp in Charlie's orchard excavated a hole deep enough to have buried a double-decker bus.

They were not averse to helping themselves to his garden produce, chicken eggs, or kisses from his entirely co-operative land girl, who admitted cheerfully that she had never had so much fun in all her life. This did not seem to upset Charlie so much as the fact that his kale field was declared a 'military area', closed off by barbed wire and patrolled by guards because the UXB boys had discovered a Hermann Goering Special giant economy-sized bomb.

Until this was defused, dismantled and taken away, Charlie could not gather fodder for his cattle. He worked himself up into a rare old state about having to beg, borrow, or even buy from friends and neighbours. It was the buying part that seemed to hurt him most.

Memories of these events speeded my undignified dash from the stalled tractor on that lovely October morning. Dad, having witnessed this, came across the fields to find out what was wrong. Telling me to stand back, he approached the plough as timorously as a fieldmouse passing a sleeping farm cat. Gently clearing the build-up of soil from the share and coulter, he lifted the cut but unburied turf, exposing part of a thick iron bar.

Convinced that no enemy aircraft was likely to have bombed us with scrap iron, we scraped and dug around, eventually uncovering an enormous spanner, about five feet long and as much as I could lift. Dad was almost certain it had been lost for almost thirty years, ever since the day the two Pennyweather brothers demonstrated their steam traction outfit's capabilities, cultivating Rest Harrow by a huge cable-hauled multi-furrowed plough, winched back and forth between two traction engines on opposite sides of the field.

There had been no love lost between the brothers, for, having decided that at well past forty it was time the pair of them settled down and married, they found that they had both been courting the same girl.

Ted won her, taking his bride and his half-share of the business across two counties, never coming back or keeping in touch with Tom again. Having left this vale of tears during the previous winter, old Tom would not be reclaiming his lost spanner. We heaved it up onto the tractor and took it back to clutter up the barn.

In common with many other local farmers who had always hired old Tom's traction-engine-driven threshing outfit, complete with itinerant work gang, Dad was wondering how we would get that year's grain threshed. The threshing machine and steam engines had stood idle behind the locked gates of Tom's yard while the legalities of his estate were sorted out. The Country War Agricultural Committee had almost draconian powers over farmers, but response to appeal for their help often seemed ponderously slow.

While we were discussing this situation, and trying to prise free the bent and broken plough share, we realized that the score of one-year-old calves we had turned out in Twelve Acres field were bellowing their heads off as if they were short of food or drink.

I knew I had filled their fifty-gallon water trough the previous afternoon, but since I had to go back to the farmyard to get a new plough share, I decided to go via Twelve Acres to see what had disturbed them, then cut along the back lane home.

Greeted by a score of ebullient young cattle who had always regarded me as an extension of their feed buckets, they pushed and barged playfully, following me to a drinking trough that was dry. By the road gate, overgrown with disuse, I noticed that something, or someone had broken down the hedge.

Scrambling through and bending bush boughs across the gap behind me, I stepped out onto the newly rolled tarmac-surfaced lane. Seeing Dick the roadman sweeping loose gravel, I knew just where the calves' drinking water had gone.

There were those of us who doubted if the lane's surface churned and rutted by the caterpillar tracks of army vehicles, would have been restored so quickly in wartime if 'The Right Hon. Frederick', known to lesser mortals as Right Orrible Fred, had not taken a tumble, ruining his smart uniform and drastically denting a 'borrowed' army motorcycle while slipping home through the lane on unofficial leave. Angrily I told Dick to deliver a message to the road-mending gang's steam roller driver, suggesting that if he needed to take our stock's drinking water to top up his tank, he was welcome to come over to our farmyard pond and take on board as much as he could swallow as I pushed him into its stagnant depths.

Dick chuckled as he lit his pipe.

'Hold hard there, girl, it wasn't us who shoved the water hose through the hedge. I was coming up to the farm at dinner time to tell you that the new engine driver of poor old Tom Pennyweather's threshing outfit has emptied the drinking water trough. I am supposed to let you know that they will be pulling into your place as soon as they finish at Four Oaks in a couple of days' time. You better be ready. It will be the back end of the winter before they are this way again.'

Still irritated about the empty trough and broken hedge, I said I would personally extend the invitation to sample our pond water to the threshing outfit driver. A curious grin spread over Dick's face as he replied that he would like to be there when I tried.

The immediate prospect of threshing the grain harvest meant that there were yards and lofts to be cleared for stacking straw and chaff, corn sacks to be mended, coal to be bought for the traction engine, and the ever-present problem of mustering sufficient help.

Three old stalwarts, Smelly Jack, Jimmy Spit and Tommy Yellows, volunteered their labour. Charlie Cartwright offered to send his land girls over to help. When Dad phoned Four Oaks Farm to ask how many hands the threshing outfit could muster, he learned there was only the driver, the bond cutter and a man who fed the opened sheaves into the revolving threshing drum. Knowing we would be short-handed, Dad phoned the County War Agricultural Committee in desperation.

A condescending female spoke of application forms requiring at least fourteen days' notice. In rather basic language Dad explained various simple aspects of farming life. A male voice intervened, saying that he would promise nothing, but would try to send some help the following day.

I was feeding sheep and cattle when the threshing outfit drew into our yard the next morning. The two dusty individuals who were wedging up wheels and adjusting drive belts were the men who had always worked with old Tom Pennyweather. The engine driver was a muscular, massive lady, whale-like in a bulging blue boiler suit and oily beret, standing over six feet tall.

My incredulous expression prompted the bond cutter to whisper that she was old Tom's niece. Her vice-like grip sent pins and needles up my arm.

'Who threatened to push me in the pond then, cheeky madam? The name is Serena. You can call me Sam!'

A hefty arm came round my shoulders as I told her of the enormous spanner we had excavated. She looked strong enough to have bent it in her teeth.

With Meg and Betty, two land army girls, and our faithful village trio in attendance, we were working desperately short-handed until a camouflaged bus came lumbering down the farm track.

'Compliments of the War Ag!' the civilian driver called, not bothering to get down from his cab. A group of dark-haired excitable young men in a variety of uniforms tumbled out of the bus, chattering together, glancing hopefully at the land girls and myself. Smelly Jack summarized the situation.

'High Tallions them are. Still classed as prisoners of war although their lot have surrendered. Not famed for overwork, and young devils with the girls.'

A good-looking young man with dark wavy hair acted as spokesman in fractured English.

'Enrico my name. Italia no longer wars with your country. Happy here to work!' The next few hours taught we girls to regard our pitchforks as weapons of defence. What with fending off Latin Romeos and Serena-Sam's heavy-handed overtures, it was a somewhat traumatic morning. After lunch break the two land girls gave fair warning that if this state of affairs continued, with Enrico the worse culprit, they would take their pinched anatomies home.

Dad was appalled at the expensively slow progress, while Serena-Sam felt concern that someone could be injured or her threshing equipment damaged. Heaving a sigh, she volunteered to try to correct the situation. Meg and Betty went to work with Jimmy Spit up on the stacked corn, leaving me as bait for hot-blooded, swaggering Enrico, so that she could cut him down to size.

I took over helping to carry sacks of wheat chaff up into the loft above the stables, and on cue, watched Serena enter the adjoining harness room, knowing she could climb up the wall rungs into the loft from there. I lingered momentarily on the outside loft step, aware that Enrico would soon be following. As a voice from the darkness above urged me to hurry, I scuttled across the loft, then descended into the harness room. As I closed the loft lid behind me, the same voice called softly, 'Enrico, over here!'

What happened after defies conjecture. Enrico eventually emerged, visibly wilting and murmuring 'Mama mia' in his distress. Serena-Sam, Nemesis in a dishevelled boiler suit, followed behind, warning that his mates would get the same treatment if they pestered we girls again.

A frantic conversation in Italian followed, and after that they all worked like Trojans. Within a week the empty barn echoed like a closed cathedral. If the old earth spirits of harvest and fertility still lingered amongst the owls and flitter bats in the high roof timbers, I wonder how they rated Enrico's encounter with Serena-Sam, an extremely strange elemental force who inspired a primeval sense of awesome fear in me.

Afternoon Surgery

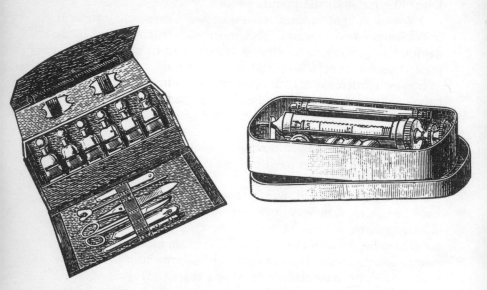

Talullah, otherwise known as Lavender Lou, plodded across the rain-soaked village green, heading towards the Post Office Stores. The impact of one mud-caked boot and her hefty shoulder set the jangling doorbell a-quiver with indignation. A potato sack slid off the bin of dog meal behind the doorway to disgorge a sudden avalanche of King Edwards across the flagstoned floor.

Totally unconcerned about the chaos she was causing, or that the postmistress was glaring thin-lipped and sour-faced as grated crab apples, Lavender Lou leaned across the marble-topped counter.

'Be this the right day and the right time, missus?' The postmistress nodded, continuing to weigh out fourteen ounces and her thumb to make a pound of currants, and deftly emptying them from the scales pan into a conical twist of blue 'sugar' paper before making a reply.

'There's a board outside the door, printed plain enough for them that care to read it, that says clear as day that the doctor's surgery is held here from three to three-thirty every second and fourth Thursday in the month.'

'I knows all that, missus!' Lavender Lou said placidly. 'But it fair do flummox folk who disremember when we get five Thursdays in a month. Be the old pill dolloper about then, for it's long gone three by the clock on the dairy cowshed?'

Somewhat defensively, the postmistress reiterated that medical men could never bank on being at one set place at a specific time. Lavender Lou stood pondering for a few seconds, summing up the situation.

'All right then, missus. Since I be yere and he ain't I might just as well go in and get his seat warm and wait for him to come.'

'Just one moment!' the postmistress called sharply, as she watched Lou tug back the curtains screening the doorway to her living quarters. 'There do be others waiting patiently to see the doctor. You must take your turn!'

'Where be they then?' Lou asked, striding across the shop to push aside the dusty cards of camphorated oil, boot laces, liver pills, and elastic that obscured her view through the steamy window. 'Be they all crouched down under your counter then, gal? There's nobbut Bob Throstle's randy old mongrel moving in the street, and, by the way, it's digging under your fence to get your yappy little lapdog. I'd be mortal 'mazed if there were ought ailing it. If there be people waiting for the doctor, where do they be hid?'

To regular, prompt-paying customers wishing to attend the doctor's surgery in her living room-cum-kitchen, the postmistress offered the grace-and-favour facility of waiting their turn for consultation in her oil-stove-heated back scullery.

The favoured (mainly female) few enjoying this advantage, ensured that no villager suffered their symptoms secretly, because every booming hearty word that the slightly deaf and elderly doctor uttered, could be clearly heard through the string-latched kitchen door.

Admission to the post office scullery was an accolade not

lightly given, and certainly not readily extended to someone as mud-caked, huge and downright awkward as Lavender Lou.

The colour of the visitor's cheeks was changing from wind-burned brown to a deepening shade of crimson as she snapped, 'I asked you, missus, where be all those folks waiting?'

There was an aggressive attitude in her stance, and in the folded arms that were capable of hoisting hundredweight sacks of pig meal up into the bran bin and, if tales told in the Horse and Harrow taproom had truth or substance, were strong enough to tuck a fourteen-stone farm hand under one elbow and thump the living daylights out of him for speaking out of turn about Lou's awesome size.

The postmistress still hesitated to answer. Even though Lavender Lou had been at Old Enery's pig farm along the back road for a couple of years, there were many doubts expressed about her status. While some villagers suggested she was Old Enery's niece, his sister, his business partner, or his mistress, the fact that neither showed the other the slightest glimmer of respect, friendship, or affection, convinced more cynical factions that she must be his legal wedded wife.

There could be no other logical reason for her to shuffle around in the mud and squalor of a derelict five-acre holding, staying with a lazy-living old rascal with no enthusiasm for work.

She was called Lavender Lou because if one had the misfortune to come into close contact with her, that fragrant country shrub was the last thing on God's earth that would spring to mind. Pigs' mess and years of boiling up coppers full of food scraps and waste offal had left an indescribable smell that surrounded her like an invisible cloud and clung to everything she touched.

She was the last person that the postmistress would willingly have invited to the inner sanctum, but she knew that an unpleasant situation could easily erupt as Lou again demanded to see where all the other patients were. Showing no joy or enthusiasm, the postmistress beckoned.

'Follow me, but mind you keep your great feet off my varnished chair stales, and first of all clean your muddy boots.' Leaving a trail of wet marks along the length of the lino-covered passage, Lou was shown into the small scullery, sharing the limited space close by the mangle with two other village matrons, not known to Lou by name.

All three sat silent around the smelly oil stove for a few seconds. Lou nodded at the heater.

'You can't beat a good old paraffin stove! Us have a couple up in Old Enery's farrowing pens and the weaner shed. I often clears off out there to stay warm and cosy after work is done for the night. It's a darn sight better than hunching over the fire when the wind us whistling through them weather-boarded walls like water through a colander. You can get mighty attached to a litter of little weaner pigs.'

Sniffing pointedly, one of the other women agreed that she was obviously deeply involved with Old Enery's pig raising. 'Ain't you flourishing with all that warmth then? I come regular with my legs, and Elsie brings her various veins when they starts throbbing, but I don't recall a great strapping wench like you ever waiting to see the doctor in here before. What ails you then?'

The flow of conversation was interrupted by an elderly gentleman who had slipped out of the back yard door on some intensely urgent business, and returned with an expression of relieved triumph on his face.

The two waiting ladies nodded understandingly, explaining in graphic detail all the problems Joe Sprockett was enduring with his 'prosperous straight gland'. The scullery was warm, and for some reason that Lou failed to understand, all three of the other waiting patients offered her first turn in the living room surgery when the doctor finally arrived. Intrigued and all agog, they listened through the closed door as the doctor asked Lou what he could do for her.

'I be here with Old Enery's back!' she confided. 'It's playing him up so rotten that he can't do a hand's turn of work!'

There was nothing strange or unusual about country men sending their womenfolk for second-hand medical advice. To lose time from work through sickness meant losing their wages. Most imagined that there was something unmanly about consulting a doctor, except as a last resort.

'Show me the area of his trouble.' The doctor's voice came clearly to the eavesdropper.

'All over,' was Lou's reply.

'You would be well advised to take a flat iron to get him moving, but, by God, something must be done about that! Come back and report without fail the next time I am here.'

There was a few seconds of whispered conversation, considered by the listeners to be a very underhand ploy. They scuttled back to their seats as Lou came through the door, silent and white-faced beneath her tan. Agreeing that Old Enery must be really sickly, they inquired of Lou if he had swine fever or suchlike, but she ignored them, too concerned about her own problems, and getting home to heat a flat iron to work on Old Enery's back.

'I don't reckon we'll bother the doctor with your throbbing veins or my legs this time,' the more garrulous patient decided. 'Cheerio,' she called to Lou. 'See you here next Thursday week!'

With the surgery over, the postmistress took the unprecedented step of removing the rag draught stoppers from her scullery window and opening the casements wide.

On the next surgery day, the two regular lady patients arrived early, ready to get the gist of Old Enery's troubles clear in their minds when Lavender Lou appeared.

She failed to show up, but shunning entry through the front shop, and without permission, Old Enery came through the back yard door and eased himself down gently beside them. He had obviously not shaved for days or changed his working clothes. The two lady patients moved away.

'You still struck bad then?'

'Bad!' he moaned. 'That silly besom came back from here with the fool advice that she'd got to take a flat iron to me to get me working. Now I've got great patches of blisters on me back. Not that she cares, the scheming great hussy. Having laid me low, she took a cartload of bacon pigs and flogged them in the market, just to pay for her to laze in hospital for weeks on end, and have an operation.

''Ain't it just like a woman to clear off, selfish like and leave me in this predicament with no one to lend a hand? Neither of you are widow women wanting a job as housekeeper, I suppose?'

There was no response to his offer, and, as if his reeking presence had some miraculously curative effect on those around him, the rest of the patients got up and went home.

He sat hunched over the oil stove until the postmistress strode in with a floor mop and a bucket of hot disinfectant.

'I'll soon cure you, you great lummox!' she scolded. 'There's you sat there stinking like a midden and moaning, while your poor housekeeper, or whatever she is supposed to be, is laying in hospital trying to recover from years of hard work and neglect. Do you want this over your head now, or will you get out of here and do some work?'

For the first time that anyone could remember, Old Enery took to his heels and ran.

Treacle Pudden

Before the artificial artery of the motorway was implanted in our rural backwater, a stony track once led to a now derelict dwelling under the woods. Penrose Pye, of indeterminate years, lived there with Bertha, his mother, and a pet pig who shared her hearthrug and his bed.

Woodman Penrose, commonly known as 'Porker', saw nothing idiosyncratic in this arrangement, affirming that no hot-water bottle matched the efficiency of his house-trained grunter for keeping his feet warm.

His pet did not give him chilblains, seldom leaked, or lost its heat before morning. Those suggesting that a pair of good woollen blankets would prove more effective and hygenic were asked to name any bedding capable of producing a litter of little pigs.

If Porker was an inept lightweight, his mother was a formidable lady who did seasonal field work on local farms. Big Bertha's

ability to charm warts gave her the reputation of having supernatural powers. If the bread dough failed to rise, settings of hens'
eggs proved infertile, or home-made wine turned vinegar sour, it
was only half in jest that some village wives would query if Big
Bertha had been upset.

Most of us rejected the idea of witchcraft. Any broomstick
Bertha mounted would have required reinforcing and case har-
dening in deference to her size. Unfettered by corsets, her
pendulous bulk was so subservient to the laws of gravity, that
tongue-in-cheek associates advised against breaking into a jog
trot because her drooping bits slapping against her could do her a
mischief as she ran.

Bertha's size and unusual domestic regime did not detract from
the fact that she was totally reliable, worked like a Trojan, and
never complained when working conditions proved unpleasant
as they did that November morning when we were gathering the
potato crop in Cold Leys.

Wet weather had delayed this task. When the ground was at
last fit to work on, I went out at daybreak with a tractor and
potato spinner, lifting the crop onto the still somewhat muddy
surface, before joining our work gang of four women who had
been putting the potatoes into sacks since eight.

A north-easterly wind carried the cutting edge of the coming
weather as it swept across the exposed muddy acres. Gathering
under a wet hedge to take a mid-morning break, we clumped
around in claybound boots.

We huddled together dressed in headscarves and macs, topped
by long hessian aprons, drinking tea from our dinner bag flasks.
At this point, less than houseproud Big Bertha suggested that
since we would probably be at the far end of our individual
potato rows by midday, she would pop home to put the kettle
and the stock pot on the stove. We could then adjourn there for
our half-hour midday break and have something wet and warm.

Somewhat squeamish, I tactfully deplored such an imposition
on her hospitality, as did a stolid dumpling of a girl named Daisy.
'Gran' Black and Dora Bramley were more forthright, bluntly
saying they had no intention of sharing Porker's pig swill. Keeping the peace, I suggested a compromise. If Bertha kindly slipped
home to get a kettle of clean water, matches and old newspaper,
Daisy could go to the end of the field and set fire to the piled-up

hedge trimmings Smelly Jack had not yet set to burn. She could put jacket potatoes in the embers and we could gather round the bonfire and warm ourselves without carting mud into Bertha's house. Daisy who had once earned Brownie badges, dashed down the field, delighted to display her campfire skills.

By midday she had conjured up a kettle of hot cocoa, toasted sandwiches and baked potatoes. We stood around appreciatively steaming in our mud-stained aprons and macs.

'You'm a good soul, Dais,' Bertha said. 'How come a good-hearted maid like you isn't wed yet?'

Regretfully, Daisy said that heading a man to the altar was like leading a horse to water. All the likely lads she knew shied away from her particular trough.

'Why don't you get friendly with my Penrose then?' Bertha enquired, adding the portentious remark: 'I want to see him settled with someone before I go.'

Wondering if Bertha had received some supernatural premonition that she was not long for this world, we glanced uneasily in her direction. She had certainly not lost weight.

Saying she had private matters to attend to early that evening, Bertha suggested Daisy might stroll over with her little dog for a bit of supper with Penrose. Hesitatingly, Daisy agreed she might walk her dog in that direction after tea. Daisy's report on her romantic encounter brightened the prospect of picking up muddy potatoes the next day.

It obviously had an extremely unpropitious start. Penrose's pet pig had objected strongly to a canine intruder, Daisy's dog having refused to relinquish a marrowbone it had found in Bertha's back yard. The animals chased each other around the room, Daisy and her host saying nothing until the squealing and barking quietened. Penrose then invited his guest to sit down. He sat down too momentarily before leaping up, squealing as loudly as his pig, and clutching himself in what Daisy called 'an unseemly manner'.

Turning slowly, he removed the marrowbone from the chair seat and flung it at the dog, saying he had lost any inclination he might have had towards finding himself a sweetheart or wife. Daisy retorted that she had not been impressed by his manners, nor those of his pet pig.

Penrose in turn pointed out that his pet did not smell, scratch out fleas, or leave bones in dangerous places. In bad times he could always eat it, which was more than Daisy could say about her dog. There the saga of Daisy and Penrose might have ended, with Daisy going home, had not Bunt Newsome's notoriously nasty donkey chosen the next few moments to go galloping down Cold Leys Lane dragging its tethering chain.

Having had the back of her coat grabbed by the biting, kicking creature, Daisy ran back to the safety of Bertha's kitchen, Penrose later walking her home. Bertha seemed extremely keen to get this unlikely couple to the altar, saying she would be happier knowing her son would be looked after when she was no longer around. Daisy, now quite amenable to the thought of marriage, confessed her ignorance of men and their 'carrying on'.

A treatise on marital bliss was expounded by our golden wed matriarch, Gran.

'What you want to do, Dais, is to give 'im plenty of Treacle Pudden made with suet, 'ot just afore bedtime. It lays 'eavy on men's stomachs and stop 'em worriting about a lot of old nonsense. If he still pesters you, try thinking of something cheerful like a dry sunny washing day, or a big tin of red salmon for Sunday tea.'

Six weeks after the encounter with Bunt Newsome's donkey, Daisy became Penrose's bride. Daisy came to work on the Monday after her Saturday morning wedding, but Bertha was absent. Solicitous enquiries were made about Daisy's newly married state.

Placidly she replied, 'Bertha couldn't go until Sunday morning. Us was pretty cramped for space on Saturday bedtime, but it would have been stupid to make sheets dirty just for one night.'

'You never slept three in a bed on your wedding night?' Gran Black asked, deeply shocked.

'More like five!' Daisy answered cheerfully. 'Him, her, me, my old dog who has always slept alongside me, and Penrose's pig. Bertha's gone now.'

'Gone where?' we asked in chorus.

Far from being past all chance of being 'pestered', Bertha had decided to act housekeeper for Bunt Newsome, a philandering horse trader who had dragged his matrimonial chain and strayed more frequently than his bad-tempered donkey, with the inevitable consequence that his long-suffering wife was no longer around to offer him all the comforts of home.

By persuading plain, unromantically inclined, titanic-sized Bertha to keep house, Bunt was trying to convince his estranged wife that he had changed his roving ways.

As Daisy related this state of affairs in the potato field that chill November morning, she called me aside confiding that there was a subject she hardly liked to mention, for fear Gran imagined Daisy had ignored her advice.

'Here, Jo,' she half whispered. 'You know Gran told me that giving Penrose treacle suet pudding for supper would keep his mind on his stomach, rather than on us being married. Well, Penrose don't eat supper, ain't partial to it, and I'm not that keen on having salmon on Sunday that I can lay dreaming about it at bedtime. I wonder if Gran knows what my Penrose does. He reckons we'd keep more cheerful cuddling up together, and, Jo, he is going to fatten up his old pig for our Christmas dinner, now he's got me to keep him warm at night.'

There seemed no adequate comment I could offer. Daisy worked on, smiling as she gathered potatoes in the muddy field.

Dora Gets Converted

Tudor ale-wives, adding seeding flowers of the wild hop weed to the beer they brewed, risked grim consequences. Such practices savoured of witch-like potions in the cauldron and was punishable by law. Such beliefs have been swept away by passing time, but hops still harbour superstition.

In those counties where the now dwindling hop-growing trade once flourished, modern innkeepers and publicans still twine hop branches across their bar-room ceilings, complying with the old belief that prosperity favours all who walk beneath the pungent-scented hop bine, and that good honest beer can be purchased at the bar.

Hop pillows are still offered as the natural answer to insomnia, with aphrodisiac qualities implied, yet much has altered since those heydays of hop picking when the soft September days brought in an influx of pale-faced town dwellers to the country on their annual rough-and-ready holiday, gathering the hops.

Most of the white-cowled, round-built oast houses, where once the hops were kilned, have been converted into quaint country residences for the more affluent among us.

A few men with their multi-purpose machines can now gather the severely restricted hop acreage in a matter of days, making the harvest a far more cost-effective proposition, and yet that vanished era brought a new dimension to those brief early autumn weeks. The slow country tempo of our lives was rent asunder by strident vitality, full of fun and fighting. Matriarchal old grannies, who pitched into each other, no holds barred, wielding their 'brollies' and jabbing with lethal-looking hatpins in the hop field, sat sharing the same quart bottle of stout, raucously singing bawdy music-hall songs together around the campfire that same night.

For those few weeks we country dwellers accepted the fact that the pale-faced puny people from the 'hopper camp' pinched plums, apples, potatoes and anything else that could be picked from a bush or tree, or dug out of the ground. Wooden fence posts were liable to find their way onto campfires. We adopted the somewhat condescending philosophy that we would probably have the same standards of behaviour if we had to live in the smoky streets of a town.

Local ladies earning a bit of 'hopping money' kept their children close by them during the first prim-lipped days of picking, but gradually the barriers of intolerance were eroded. The townsfolk realized that country clodhoppers were as sharp-witted as themselves, although they might make less noise about it.

We learned that the poor and underprivileged needed to have a very special kind of courage to survive their poverty-stricken city environment with pride. Shared sorrow brought the two factions closer. When a small child was so terribly burned by a faulty spirit stove that her parents kept constant vigil at her hospital bedside for over a fortnight, a village wife took care of the remaining children and everyone in the hop field voluntarily emptied part of their pickings into the parents' tally bin to give them financial support.

The hop fields frequently echoed with laughter. They certainly did that September morning when Dora Slogg started

hollering and screeching that she had just received a message
from the sky. Doughty Dora was a substantially built matron
whose body resembled stacked layers of large motor-lorry tyres at
various stages of inflation.

As a regular seasonal occupant of the hoppers' huts for as long
as most of us could remember, Dora seemed to bring a new three-
month-old baby with her every time she came. That year her
family was just one short of a round dozen. This gave the more
earthy types an almost inexhaustible supply of verbal ammuni-
tion, making jokes about Dora's home-grown football side, or her
cricket eleven, with allusions to the likelihood of producing a
twelfth man for her team.

Dora was not one to stand too much taunting. Her brawny
partner, 'Brussels', knew that there were limits to Dora's temper
beyond which he would not personally care to go. Prior to her
'wondrous revelation', Dora's behaviour gave no hint of the
serene seraphic personality change that was to come. She had
certainly been her normal quarrelsome self the previous morning
in the hop field.

Two cloth-capped and caustic-tongued ladies in the next hop
alley were discussing the fact that most of Dora's swarm of children had Junetide birthdays. Counting nine months backwards
on hop-stained fingers, they concluded that Dora and Brussels
must have been particularly susceptible to the notoriously stimulating effect of the hops.

To have crowned one of the conversationalists soundly on the
head with an eight-pint-size iron saucepan was a bit much, even
by hop field standards, but to have tipped it up over her and her
companion, was considered to be 'disgusting', seeing that it was
full of cold boiled chitterlings in onion gravy at the time.

The two victims shrieked with temper. The Slogg children's
dinner may have looked like chopped up bits of cycle inner tub-
ing, but they howled to see it spilling on the dirt.

At that time, evangelical missioners used to visit the hop field
on a daily basis, and despite all the mocking attitudes the pickers
affected, it was recognized that these young men did sterling
work. No task was too menial. They helped with the pickers'
problems and had a working knowledge of first aid.

When one of the smaller Sloggs developed an abscessed tooth
that made him bawl all night long, rendering the whole hoppers'

camp sleepless, a Brother John volunteered to take the child for treatment, walking the twelve-mile-round journey with the swollen-faced small lad on his back.

It was Brother John who intervened when the saucepan-crowning incident seemed liable to develop into a feud. By quietly picking up the offending saucepan, gathering up the chitterlings and offering them around to all the contenders, he brought about a lull in the hostilities, and within a few minutes anger was replaced by smiles.

Brother John and another missioner sat picking hops into Dora's tally bin. Two extra pairs of hands helped raise the Sloggs' tally of picked hops to the highest daily number recorded in the Tally Master's book.

Dora spent a reasonably peaceful evening sharing gossip and the warmth of the campfire with the other women pickers, but when Brussels staggered back from the village inn full of 'singing beer' and somewhat maudlin, her shrill-voiced invective led to a public fist fight between them before they retired to continue a private battle in their overcrowded hut.

Trailing across the dew-wet grass to start work the following morning, Dora suddenly started hollering and waving her arms in the air like a soul demented. Those nearest to her came to the conclusion that she had been stung by a wasp.

'No I ain't, you daft beggars,' Dora snorted. 'Go fetch that young preacher fella, someone. Tell him I've just heard voices from the sky!'

Stifled sniggers and sneers of open derision greeted this announcement. One kindly intentioned picker, concluding that Dora was hysterical, tried to administer shock treatment, her restorative remedy consisting of a bunch of wet dock leaves thrust down the back of Dora's dress. In normal circumstances this would have been an open invitation to a black eye, but on that September morning Dora smiled seraphically.

'I know you mean well, dearie, and I forgive all you other jeering suspicious sinners. It is not your faults if you've all been raised as coarse as the sacking aprons around your waists.'

Listening to Dora's newly found placidity, the group gathered around her decided it might be as well if Brother John was summoned to help her, for the poor soul had obviously gone clean off her head.

Brother John and his group of young evangelist helpers came to the alley where Dora and her children were gathering the first cold wet hops of the day. They sat picking hops and discussing Dora's strange experience, somewhat disconcerted by her obvious change of attitude.

Cynical pickers suggested that Dora had thought up a highly original way to attract volunteers to help fill her tally bin. Others felt there was something strange at work in the hop field. The atmosphere was unusually subdued.

Sensing this reaction, Brother John realized that this was a perfect opportunity to gather stray sheep into his fold. He started by tactfully enquiring if Dora's latest infant had been baptized, suggesting that he might hold an open-air service around the hop yard campfire the following Sunday afternoon. Dora meekly said she would consider his proposal and hoped they could discuss the situation in some depth. This meant that for the next couple of days Dora's hop alley was picked and cleared away ahead of the rest.

Brussels was none too cheerful about the situation. Although Dora's voices in the sky had supposedly told her to be charitable towards her neighbours, very little of her charity came his way. By the fourth day Brother John was beginning to doubt Dora's motives, but that astute lady shattered his disbelief with one remark.

'Well, sonny, if you're going to "do" the nipper on Sunday, we will get the whole lot of them done together. I'd expect "naming" all eleven to come cheaper than dipping them one at a time!'

The enthusiastic missioner arranged a 'Service of Celebration', with a hop pickers' party to follow. Eleven little Sloggs were scrubbed and polished and brought forward somewhat reluctantly, a china washbowl serving as a font.

All peaceable and overflowing with the milk of human kindness, Dora interrupted the singsong that followed, to make a little speech.

'After the grand job Brother John has done with my kids this afternoon, I'm wondering if he would get me married all legal and proper like, while we're down here in the country, I'd like to get it all tidied up at once!'

Brussels, having the grace to blush, went back to town that evening, but Dora's wedding was arranged for the last Saturday of the hopping season, at the village church. She drew an advance on her hop-picking money for a new dress and a frizzy perm. The church was packed with pickers and village folk, all interested in witnessing the wedding of the parents of eleven children.

Brussels arrived sporting a cabbage rose in his buttonhole and a new white choker round his neck. He was accompanied by a timid-looking little man dressed in a shiny blue suit several sizes too large for him. They stood together by the altar steps, Brussels standing at the other man's right hand. Dora strolled up the aisle with her entire brood trailing behind her.

Brother John, assisting the village parson, pointed out that the bridegroom and best man were standing in the wrong places, Brussels should be standing beside Dora.

'Not ruddy likely!' Dora giggled, forgetting her new-found gentility. 'Old Brussels is my Alf's best man. He's been our next-door neighbour for years.'

Any further remarks from Brother John were swiftly silenced by Dora's elbow, and her explanation.

'Hops bring my Alf out in a rash, so Brussels comes on holiday to help me and the kids to earn a bit of hop-picking money. Is there anything wrong in that?'

There seemed to be no adequate answer. The service was short, sharp, and simple. The 'knees up' atmosphere of the party that followed in the hop yard was in no way diminished by the fact that Dora's Alf slipped quietly away and went back to town. As Dora said, hops brought him out in a rash and he knew that Brussels was there to look after her and the kids!

The Calico Bonnet

Asoutherly breeze came whispering across the lonely
coastal marshes, sweeping the trailing fringe of grey mist
back into the cold murky depths of the North Sea. A
colony of nesting sea terns rose up from the sparse grass out along
the estuary saltings, screaming and circling as Sally Hulver
walked amongst them with her long-tined rake and heavily laden
cockle basket on her arm.

Having been out along the shore since first light of dawn, she
paused to rest momentarily, enjoying the new-found warmth of
the strengthening sun.

Placid ripples of an incoming tide lapped along the shore line
as innocently as beguiling kittens, gently transforming the
treacherous mudflats into a sparkling sheet of sunbright water.
All Sally's seventeen years had been spent within the sound of
the waves. She knew that such tranquillity could be dangerously

deceptive. The moods of the sea altered so quickly, each lapping kitten wavelet becoming a ravenous beast of prey, hurling breakers inshore, rushing to engulf those who ventured across the vast expanse of the mudflats after the turn of the tide, covering the beach faster than a man might run.

When the spring tides came, there could be as much as a mile of viscid silt and shingle between high tide and low water. Sally had walked along this inhospitable stretch of the estuary coastline most days of her life since early childhood, but there had still been three occasions when she had been so intent on gathering shellfish in the shallows, she had failed to notice that the unpredictable sea was infiltrating across the beach beside and behind her.

Each time, she had floundered through deepening water and stumbled ashore exhausted, soaked to the skin, and almost as afraid of going home to face her father with an empty cockle basket as of getting herself drowned.

With the nearest human habitation more than a mile away, home for Sally was a comfortless, squat, stone-built, single-storey dwelling huddled under the landward side of the sea wall that protected the sheep-dotted marshes from inundation along the bleak estuary coast.

Birds by the thousand over-wintered or raised their young out amongst the sea lavender and coarse grasses of the saltings. Watching the furious aerobatic sea terns, the raucous swooping gulls, the dunlins and little plovers scurrying busily along the tideline, Sally envied them the feathers covering their faces, and their ability to fly wherever they chose.

As the skinny, forlorn-looking girl stood lost in thought among the innumerable mottled eggs lying in inadequate grass-scrape nests, the distracted sea terns swooped low enough for their wingtips and claws to brush against the calico bonnet on her head.

Sally's clearest memory of early childhood was of birds eggs. Abel and Zeke, her twin older brothers, had filled their caps with eggs they had found in a mallard's nest along the sea wall, their brow-beaten mother deciding this offering was a cause for celebration. In their miserable little dwelling under the sea wall, such plenitude was extremely rare.

Sally remembered still the tense anticipation as her mother

quickly transformed the mallard eggs into fluffy, slightly fishy-tasting pancakes, cooked on an iron skillet and topped with a dollop of black treacle. This impromptu feast had to be eaten quickly, for fear that their fisherman father returned unexpectedly from his crab pots and lines out in the estuary, and caught them loitering at home instead of raking shellfish from the beach on the ebb tide. Then as now, Jericho Hulver in a temper was terrible to behold.

Apart from that one illicit feast, Sally's recollection of pre-school days conjured up only grey misty images of having to haul an old pram on runners out on the mudflats, the bone-chilling, numb-fingered misery of trailing tiny hands through cold sea water, picking up the shellfish her mother raked from the desolate wind-scoured beach.

Sally remembered no word of affection or encouragement ever being offered to his wife or children by Jericho Hulver, no matter how heavily the old pram was laden as they hauled it home.

Fear had always stalked through the humpback cottage whenever her father was in the house, the tension only lessening on the days when he sailed the twelve miles down the coast to the quayside market of a small fishing port to sell his harvest from the sea. The length of his absence depended on the state of the tides, weather conditions, and, as Sally now suspected, the company he kept in the Sceptre of Neptune inn close by the harbour wall.

On these trips, Jericho always purchased the meagre household supplies he considered to be necessary. Sally's mother having no choice in the matter, or money in her purse. Time had not softened Jericho Hulver's tyrannical attitude or changed the insularity of a life style that discouraged all contact with those who dwelt in the scattered hamlets on the landward side of the marsh.

Sally had first discovered the big wide world beyond the marsh tracks when officialdom decreed that she was of an age to accompany her twin brothers on their two-mile trudge to a marsh-side village school. Abel and Zeke, then aged eleven, were hardly ecstatic at the prospect of accompanying their apprehensive little sister along dyke-side marsh tracks and a stony path along the edge of a mud-silted tidal creek. This emerged at the lower end of the village to join a tarred road with a pavement alongside. On Sally's first morning as a school pupil, she had dawdled along in wonderment at so smooth a surface beneath her boots.

Answering the clanging of the summoning school bell. Abel and Zeke had abandoned their little nuisance sister, rather than risk being late. Time to Sally was allied to the tides. She saw no cause to hurry. In this hitherto undiscovered place were cottage gardens full of beautiful scented flowers. Smiling women in pretty pinafores had time to stand chatting and laughing together at the school gate.

A man in a straw hat and striped apron had paused from adjusting a shop blind to ask if it was her first day at school. He then gave her a bar of sticky toffee, treasured in memory and licked sparingly for days.

This then was a place where men spoke without shouting or hitting, where women had pretty hair and neat polished shoes, a unique experience for the undersized five-year-old daughter of a tyrannical father and a partially crippled mother, living in the poverty-stricken hovel under the sea wall.

Here on her first morning at school came Sally's searing agony of discovering that she was not like other children – a deformed freak, totally rejected by the taunting pupils swarming round her in the playground, calling her cruel names. She still recalled the anguish of vainly crying for her brothers to come and rescue her. Maybe it was in that first moment of terrified bewilderment that she realized she would always have to fight her nightmare situation alone.

Having settled the rest of the pupils to lessons in the communal schoolroom, the school mistress had taken her misfit intake infant to the brown stone sink in the entrance lobby to bathe Sally's tear-stained face. At home water had to be carried by shoulder yoke and bucket, the artesian well, from which old sailing ships had taken on supplies of sweet fresh water, at least a quarter-mile away along the sea wall. There at school, the teacher could make water flow by simply turning a big brass tap.

There for the first time Sally had seen her own frightening reflection in a damp-mottled mirror. She still recalled the sensation of running an exploring finger around the outline of a dark blemish staining her cheek from temple to jaw line, making her face look lopsided. The 'School Miss' had untied Sally's tight-plaited braids, combing her hair forward to hang like a curtain around her face.

'Other pupils will soon become accustomed to your unfortunate birthmark, child. Dry your eyes. Few people on this earth are without some personal cross to bear.'

Belying this stoical approach, the teacher sent Sally home with a parcel when that first day of school life was over. This contained a jar of lanolin, and some remnants of calico to which she had pinned the paper pattern for a deep-brimmed sun bonnet. An accompanying note informed Sally's mother that her daughter would now be expected to wear the finished article every time she attended school.

Thankful that Jericho Hulver had chosen that evening to take his boat out night-fishing for the cod that were being caught beyond the wide mouth of the estuary, Sally's mother stitched by candlelight long past her husband's usual curfew demand that no lamp oil or candle wax be wasted after nine o'clock.

Sally wore her new calico bonnet when she set off to school with Abel and Zeke the following morning. The deep buckram-lined brim almost encircled her face, restricting sideways vision, but effectively shielded her left cheek from the tormenting stares of other schoolchildren, and from the incessant, skin-chapping wind. Apart from minor adaptions of size and available material, the style of headgear Sally had first worn as a tear-stained five-year-old had altered little ever since.

Twelve years later, now a timid seventeen-year-old girl carrying her harvest of cockles home to her tyrant father, she still wore a cotton bonnet to hide her birthmarked face.

Sally's schooldays had been a terrifying ordeal, endured under threat of an awful monster called an 'Attendance Officer', who would otherwise lock her up in a dungeon, deep and dark. Fragmentary bits and pieces of rudimentary education washed over her as she sat in the same desk in the back row of the communal classroom, much as driftwood floats ashore on an incoming tide. On occasion, the 'nit nurse' came examining heads with a sharp-pointed knitting needle. Sally was always called out last to have her hair searched in the coat lobby, the only occasion during school hours she was allowed to remove her bonnet.

At one point that memory refused to specify, this antiseptic-smelling lady in her rustling stiff-starched apron held court in the front room of the school ma'am's house, where an elderly, sleepy-looking doctor sat at a table behind a screen.

Sally recalled that she had taken very little interest in this cursory medical examination, her attention being totally engrossed by the pale patterned wallpaper, the floral window curtains, a huge vase of sweet-scented flowers, and brass ornaments gleaming in the light of a banked-up log fire. She had never imagined that so beautiful a room could have existed, much less that it was situated just beyond the school yard.

The letter Sally was given that afternoon had been addressed to her father, but he was out baiting his crab pots in the estuary when she went home. Being afraid to open the envelope and ascertain the contents, Sally's downtrodden mother asked anxiously if the nurse or doctor had questioned Sally about her birthmark, or any bruises she might have. Sally's truthful reply that she had not really been taking much notice of what they were saying, had aggravated her mother's agitated state.

The momentary expression of furtive fear that crossed her father's face as he picked up the letter, remained clearly imprinted in Sally's memory, even if it had vanished as he tore the envelope apart.

'Bloody poke-nosing interfering busybodies!' he had blustered as colour returned to his cheeks. He flung the letter across the room. 'I'm of a mind to go and tell that high and mighty school ma'am and that meddling doctor where to put their charity. The snivelling kid must have gone whimpering, whining and telling lies. I can look to my own without them sticking their snouts in where they're not wanted! They'll get short shrift if they come round here. They've got the brass-faced nerve to say she's undersized and undernourished, so they've sent a form entitling her to free jars of cod liver oil, for God's sake! If they're supposed to be educated people, wouldn't you think that the thick-skulled fools would realize that the last thing we go without here is fish!'

Even as young schoolboys, Sally's wiry twin brothers had been expected to bait lines, mend nets and refill the wooden holding butts of gathered live shellfish with a change of sea water twice a day. A few months before his sons left school, Jericho Hulver acquired a larger boat, leaky, paint-starved, and long past its prime. Every waking moment of the boys' lives had been geared by their father into making the old fishing vessel seaworthy, hull scraping, caulking timbers, and applying coats of boiling pitch. Domineering as ever, Jericho Hulver never questioned but that

Abel and Zeke would crew for him. His family had sailed this lonely treacherous coast for generations.

The twins had reluctantly complied with his demand, having less respect for their father than for the buckle end of his leather belt.

Now Sally went to school alone. The haunting memory of those terrifying solo journeys through marsh mist, filldyke rain, frost, gales, and winter dark, remained deep-etched in her conscious mind, and still troubled her sleep at times. Throughout her schooldays, she had been the butt of ignorance, an object of ridicule to schoolroom peers.

She had loathed the patched outgrown clothes on her back, her disfigured face, the awful heavy workman-style boots her father had bought at least three sizes too large so that they would last until she was full-grown.

During that time, Sally began to realize that despite a brutish father, an intimidated, increasingly immobile mother, and twin brothers who tended to ignore her, the isolation of the wide windswept wetlands, the dangerous coast and remoteness of her home under the sea wall brought solitude and sanctuary from the mocking hostile world beyond the marsh. The incident causing the culmination of her schooldays occurred three months before her fourteenth birthday.

During a needlework lesson on that autumn Friday afternoon, Sally had failed to understand the procedure by which she was supposed to shape the heel of a knitted sock. Her usual method of avoiding confrontation with a small group of taunting bullies had been to slip away quickly as soon as lessons were over, then head for home as fast as her clumsy loose boots would allow. That afternoon she had to stay behind and sort out the cat's cradle of wool that in no way resembled anything to cover a foot.

After the imposed extra knitting session, she became aware that her two main adversaries and a sycophant crowd of followers had congregated just beyond the school gate. Big Ronnie stood almost six feet tall and about half as wide, a loutish foul-mouthed boy, prone to using small creatures as target practice for his catapult. Pimply faced sadistic Len, Ronnie's sidekick, frequently terrified other pupils into handing over the meagre contents of their dinner bags. Sally had often gone hungry to satisfy his greed.

She had known there would be no hope of avoiding the jeering crowd as soon as Ronnie's equally unpleasant sister saw her crossing the yard.

'Here she is! Old Toad Face in her rag hat! Our Dad says she shouldn't be allowed to come here to school. He says them swampies from out across the marsh were all born with webbed feet, just like frogs. That's why she has to wear such kipper-box boots. Let's take them off her to look, then throw them in the pond.'

The shouted response to this suggestion had been instantaneous, as noisy as a pack of baying hounds in full cry, with Sally the unfortunate fox. She had darted back across the yard in panic. A wooden panel that served to screen the insalubrious girls' lavatory from the inquisitive gaze of precocious boys, shielded her as she headed towards a last-resort escape route she had previously noticed but never felt desperate enough to try.

No clear memory remained of actually plunging through the vicious sharp spikes of a thick blackthorn hedge. All she recalled was a sensation of total helplessness as she skittered down the steep, wet, slippery grass embankment on the other side, colliding with a woman wearing a blue floral apron over a huge egg-shaped stomach, sending the woman's older companion tumbling with her, all three of them falling like skittles on a muddy bridle path.

Sally's cotton bonnet had been knocked askew as her face brushed against the fat person, who sat up screaming. The older woman hauled Sally to her feet.

'You wicked clumsy freak! Do you want her child to be cursed with the devil's hoof mark on its face, the same as yours is? And her at full term too! Get back to the godforsaken place where you belong. Leave decent folk alone.'

A slap across the face sent Sally running until she was safely out across the marsh.

Big Ronnie and his sister grabbed her as she hurried into the school yard just as the assembly bell was ringing on that following Monday morning. Kicking, punching, they told her that she was likely to be sent to prison because their aunt had given birth to a dead baby with a huge deformed head. After morning prayers, the school mistress took Sally into the schoolhouse living room and asked what had occurred on the previous Friday afternoon.

She had been very kind, admitting her belief that Sally's scramble through the hedge had been caused by intolerable bullying.

While reassuring Sally that the birthmark on her face had absolutely no connection with the deformities of the dead baby, the teacher warned that she might well encounter ignorant unpleasantness from a few superstitious people and their children. With this situation in mind, and at total variance to all the rules and regulations, the school mistress thought it best to send Sally home at once, by reason of a mythical rash that would keep her away in isolation for at least the next two weeks.

As it happened, Sally needed no excuses for her absence from lessons. The autumn equinox brought storm-force winds and mountainous seas to pound the coast, the combination of spring tides and on-shore winds forcing more water up into the estuary. Gigantic waves hurled themselves up over the saltings, sending spray and spume flying high over the sea wall, lashing down on the cottage roof.

Low tide that afternoon found the mudflats still covered with white-capped water. Jericho said that they would be lucky if their shirts stayed dry all night.

In the raging wind, torrential rain, and gathering darkness, Abel, Zeke and Sally helped their father winch-haul the boat up over the sea wall, securing it to two deep-driven posts on the marsh side of the house.

The fury of the wind increased as the tide rose, the roaring sea a monstrous beast of prey, hurling itself at the flimsy barricade of the sea wall, greedily seeking to devour them all. Bundling bedding, boxes and odd bits of furniture up through the narrow hatchway of the loft that had served as the twins' sleeping quarters, Sally watched sea water begin to cover the stone floor. Her mother was far too arthritic to clamber up the loft ladder. Abel and Zeke lifted her onto a chair placed on the kitchen table before going aloft with their father, calling to Sally to hurry up the ladder before the water rose.

She had looked at her mother, so frail and frightened, and put another chair on the table to stay and keep her company. Transcending all the remembered noise and terror of that night of the flood, was the very precious memory of her mother half whispering about matters she had never mentioned before. Sitting with the water lapping against the table legs beneath them, her Mum had talked of her own girlhood, a spoilt headstrong miss whose wealthy parents had rented a quayside cottage for a fortnight, a pert summer visitor who had paid a masterful-looking young fisherman to row her along the estuary coast for a picnic.

In turn he had been paid to marry her in haste a couple of months later, Sally's now-dead grandparents having ordered their disgraced daughter out of their house and out of their lives. With hindsight, Sally now thought that perhaps her mother had some kind of premonition on that terrifying night.

Low water had at dawn found Sally wading knee-deep across the kitchen, the marsh beyond the sea-salt-stained window one vast lake. As the wind died down, the weather turned much colder and the flood slowly receded. Cleaning the aftermath of mud and shingle from the sea-saturated dwelling left Sally and her mother totally exhausted. Little help was forthcoming from her father and brothers because they were trying to make the storm-damaged boat seaworthy enough to sail down the coast for essential supplies. The cold and damp gave Sally's mother a bronchial-sounding cough that troubled her night and day.

The great storm had washed many interesting objects ashore. After it abated, Sally was sent beachcombing for this harvest from the sea. She piled this up in heaps for the twins to collect later, and dragged the lighter bits of driftwood home.

Towards noon one morning, while Sally was out along the shore, her father had gone indoors and found his wife asleep in her chair. Shouting and shaking failed to wake her. Zeke and Abel eventually convinced him that their mother was unconscious and very sick indeed.

With the cottage still virtually isolated from the nearest village by the inundated marsh, Jericho decided to wrap his wife in a blanket and sail down the coast to the fishing town before the tide ebbed. There she could receive free medical help. Sally saw the boat heading down the estuary as she returned laden with driftwood. She never saw her mother again.

It had been taken for granted that she would now cook, clean and housekeep for her father and brothers. Her father, temporarily chastened, soon became more domineering and bad-tempered than before. Only along the foreshore with her cockle rake and basket had Sally found some measure of peace. The impending threat of a second world war had made little impact on Jericho Hulver's menage until the twins, then almost twenty, found enough courage to tell their father they had signed on to join the Merchant Navy.

Purple with rage, Jericho had called them terrible names, telling them to go and never come back again. Still swearing, he had rowed away to inspect his crab lines. Watching his father out across the water, Abel went into the store room and came back into the kitchen with a bottle of brandy. Sally had asked where it came from.

'Don't act daft as well as damaged,' he had answered, laughing. 'You would know that the old man sometimes hauls in more profitable catches than crabs and lobsters if you didn't hide inside the blasted cloth bonnet that you stick on your head.'

Much to Sally's surprise, Zeke argued in her defence.

'There's no call to bawl at Sal. Her damaged face is not her fault, Abe! She's suffered more than us. We both know the truth. We know that we'll not be here for the old man to belt us silly as he's done since that day when she was a bawling baby, but Sal has nowhere else to go.'

Sally stood silent and puzzled as Zeke continued to have his say.

'Listen, Sal, I don't like leaving you to be the butt of the old man's tempers. If he starts getting rough-handed, ask him to tell you about the evening Mum was boiling a pan of cockles and you were teething. Just ask him about that!'

As the twins left home, Abel put a brotherly arm around her shoulders, Zeke actually kissed her clumsily on her good cheek. She was not to know then that this first show of their affection towards their younger sister was to be the last in their war-shortened, torpedoed lives.

With his sons now merchant seamen, Jericho had become more morose and unpredictable. The outbreak of war brought some restrictions to his fishing activities. Naval vessels hurried up and down the estuary. There were occasional army exercises on the marsh, and a noisy anti-aircraft gun site down the coast. Many battles were fought in the skies overhead, yet the brown-sailed barges still plied placidly up and down the coast.

A Royal Observer Corps post had been set up in a camouflaged blockhouse a mile or so along the sea wall beyond the cockle beds, but Sally saw little of those who manned it.

In fact as she stood in the warm spring sunshine remembering the past, she realized that her contacts with the world beyond the marsh since her schooldays could almost be numbered on the fingers of her hand. Thinking of days that had gone brought no echoes of happiness or laughter, and who could tell about the future? She had lingered daydreaming far too long.

As she picked up her cockle basket, she saw something she first thought to be a seal bobbing among the wavelets about a hundred and fifty yards offshore. Her second glance made her realize that this was something far more lethal. She turned and ran back along the sea wall to the Observer Corps lookout post as fast as her legs would carry her, to warn of the floating mine that had drifted inshore.

A middle-aged, uniformed man rushed out to meet her. As he made the necessary urgent phone calls, his companion told Sally to rest a while to recover her breath, offering her a cup of tea from his flask. This cheerful individual's lopsided face bore a deep scarred dent across his forehead and down one cheekbone, but this did not seem to bother him at all.

Both men were probably much the same age as her father, but were kind and considerate, telling her that they often saw her at work along the shore through their field glasses. In fact she had become a kind of mascot to everyone manning that post. Other coastal sections had identifying emblems of birds of prey and suchlike. Theirs was the black silhouette of a young lady in a sun bonnet with rake and basket on her arm.

After the day that she saw the mine, she somehow felt less lonely. Now when the plane spotters from the lookout post waved in greeting from a distance, she waved back.

During that summer, the scar-faced man occasionally walked along the beach for a chat as she gathered cockles, telling of his pilot son, and his three grown daughters. He told her of the piece of red-hot shrapnel that had carved through his face during the First World War, and of the nightmare days that came after, with him wanting to hide away from the rest of the world. He spoke of the recent, almost miraculous medical advances in plastic surgery, and reminded her that the lookout post was manned day and night if she ever needed help.

Afterwards Sally wondered if the 'spotters' had heard about her father's violent tempers, or had observed his strange behaviour from afar. Several times of late he had rowed his catch down to the quayside market and come back without even their basic food ration and supplies, then grumbled at the expense. She was quite convinced that his mind was deteriorating on that calm September afternoon when he insisted that a terrible storm was brewing, declaring that he must row out to haul in his crab lines and prevent the creels getting smashed.

The sea was still as calm as a stagnant marsh ditch as he pulled away from the rickety wood-planking landing stage. Within half an hour a ferocious rip tide surged up through the estuary in a freak storm that ended as quickly as it had begun. Wreckage from his boat washed ashore two days later, but Jericho's body was never found. The sea had claimed him, just as it had taken his twin sons.

For days Sally existed in a dreamlike state where nothing seemed real except the silence. She found herself listening for the sound of the boat being winched up the shingle, and the clump of her father's sea boots on the wooden landing stage.

She did not weep or mourn him. Any tears she shed were still for her misused Mum. Eventually she faced the task of sorting through her father's possessions. While clearing out the cluttered wall cupboard by the chimney breast in what had been his bedroom, she found an old newspaper cutting.

Under the heading 'Royal Yacht Anchors in Estuary' was a photo of a flag-waving group of watchers along the sea wall. In the foreground were Abel and Zeke as little lads, alike as peas from the same pod. Their mother stood beside them. The baby cradled in her arms had round dimpled cheeks with no sign of a birthmark. Zeke's parting words came out of the past.

'Ask him to tell you about the evening Mum was boiling a pan of cockles and you were teething.'

The unbidden tears Sally shed at that moment were fuelled by rage. Furiously turfing out bits and pieces that her father had hoarded, she realized that the wooden back of the cupboard seemed to be loose. It came away with a hefty tug and a poker used as a lever. In the cavity behind, she found a wash-leather bag filled with golden sovereigns and wads of banknotes wrapped in oilskin.

A bundle of legal papers established that under the joint wills of her wealthy maternal grandparents, all monies raised in the disposal of their estate had been left in trust for her mother's children until they reached the age of twenty-one. The interest this capital accrued was to be credited to her mother annually. This tallied with her father's savings account book figures, which now stood at an amazingly substantial sum.

It was obvious that she was comparatively wealthy and yet as Sally stood taking stock of the situation, she could only think of her mother who never had a spare penny in her purse, and had almost needed to grovel before her husband would spend coppers to replace the darned, worn-out socks on his children's feet.

She returned all the money and papers to their hiding place behind the false back of the cupboard, then went along the sea wall to seek the advice of her battle-scarred spotter friend at the lookout post. That night she stitched herself a new bonnet.

A pre-dawn start and a long train journey to see a city hospital consultant confirmed what she already suspected. Her facial blemish had been caused by scalding, but he was convinced that, given time, patience and money, most of the damage was reparable. Sally assured him she had all three.

She had watched the sea cover the beach every day for as long as she could remember. Now she was leaving. Her craggy-faced Royal Observer Corps friend and his gentle wife had trundled across the marsh tracks in a borrowed Austin Seven. Still mourning their dead pilot son, they had found room in their hearts to offer her sanctuary in their home.

She walked out to the edge of the sea with the gulls screaming their goodbyes around her. Slowly undoing the strings of her bonnet, she flung it into the tide. The wind wrapped her long hair around her face as she retraced her steps.

'That peekaboo hairstyle is all the rage. You are a really lovely-looking girl,' the sad-eyed woman told her, somehow reminding Sally of her old teacher on that first day she went to school.

The door of the damp dilapidated cottage stood ajar, her cockle rake leaning against the wall beside it. Sally hurried into the car with never a backward glance.